A Year in the Life

The Journals of Michelle Wright

Michelle Wright's discography

Do Right By Me
Michelle Wright
Now & Then
The Reasons Why
For Me It's You
The Greatest Hits Collection
Shut Up and Kiss Me
A Wright Christmas

www.michelle-wright.com
email: ayearinthelife@michelle-wright.com

A Year in the Life
The Journals of Michelle Wright

Michelle Wright

INSOMNIAC PRESS

Library and Archives Canada Cataloguing in Publication

Wright, Michelle, 1961-
A year in the life. The Journals of Michelle Wright / Michelle Wright.

ISBN 1-894663-81-0

1. Wright, Michelle, 1961- 2. Country musicians--Canada--Diaries.
I. Title.

ML420.W952A3 2005   782.421642'092   C2005-900245-X

The publisher gratefully acknowledges the support of the Canada Council, the Ontario Arts Council and the Department of Canadian Heritage through the Book Publishing Industry Development Program.

Printed and bound in Canada

Insomniac Press
192 Spadina Avenue, Suite 403
Toronto, Ontario, Canada, M5T 2C2
www.insomniacpress.com

The Canada Council | Le Conseil des Arts
FOR THE ARTS | DU CANADA
SINCE 1957 | DEPUIS 1957

ONTARIO ARTS COUNCIL
CONSEIL DES ARTS DE L'ONTARIO

To my mother, Monica Wright.
Thank you for always being there for me when I needed you.

Introduction

I've been keeping a journal on and off for about eight years now. When I was asked if I'd be interested in doing one for a full year of my life and then sharing it with the public, I thought it might be fun and interesting to undertake. I then became nervous because I knew it would mean opening up my life to everyone. Having been approached about writing an autobiography, but knowing I'm just not ready for that yet, I decided this book might be the next best thing, perhaps giving me a taste of what writing an autobiography would be like.

Well, I must admit that the discipline and diligence required to keep this journal was quite challenging at times. I also became concerned about whether or not the activities of my daily life were really all that interesting. But after rereading these entries, I recognize that I have had the privilege of sharing with you a very good and positive time in my life.

I've described the everyday activities involved in running the Convertino household, and I've detailed the continual joys and challenges of being a recording artist.

While I don't claim to be an expert on how to deal with every aspect of life's journey, all of the challenges that I have had to confront (and there have been many, but I'm saving them for the autobiography) have helped me to create the kind of life that I live today: happy, varied, and balanced—as the girl on the road and as the wife at home. Quite frankly, I find my life to be pretty simple and satisfying; at times it's all-consuming, but generally a joy. I believe my contentment has a lot to do with the level of maturity I have attained at this point in my life, and how well-suited Marco and I are for each other. (Who you choose to be your significant other makes a big difference in what your life looks like.) Furthermore, including God in my life and reading the Bible has made my life and the decisions I make so much better. It's the peace that passes understanding. I highly recommend it.

I hope you enjoy a few laughs as you read on, and I hope I can be an inspiration on some level, too.

Love,

Michelle Wright

January 1st

I always love to celebrate the start of the new year, and Marco and I did it in style this New Year's Eve. We stayed at home and Marco made his famous Convertino pasta sauce. Marco is a New York Italian and his family's marinara recipe is the best I have ever tasted. We started the fireplace, turned on the Christmas lights, lit the candles, and had a total movie marathon night. We watched *Owning Mahoney* with Philip Seymour Hoffman. We like this actor. He plays a Canadian with a gambling problem. We also watched *White Christmas* and *It's a Wonderful Life*. (We usually watch *White Christmas* on Christmas Day, but we had Marco's sister Celeste and brother-in-law Pat over for Christmas. They have just moved to Nashville from L.A. We had a great time together playing games and hanging out.) Anyhow, back to our movie marathon. I used to be unable to sit still long enough to enjoy more than about one movie, but Marco has had a very calming effect on me and I have learned how to appreciate the value of relaxing. Then we ate red velvet cake with ice cream until we couldn't eat anymore. It was glorious.

Now here comes 2004. I also believe in making New Year's resolutions. I quit smoking on New Year's Eve eight years ago. Mind you, it took me a few New Year's Eves to lick that one. But I did, and I highly recommend it. I started cutting back a few months before and then I used the nicotine patch when I needed it because there is some serious withdrawal that happens and I think it's important to use what is available to help you through. So this year is no exception when it comes to resolutions. I, like millions of other people out there, will be attempting to get back into the gym more often and just take better care of myself. But for the rest of the holidays, we will be continuing to lie around and enjoy. "Commence-O Festival" as Marco likes to say.

January 2nd

Still lying around talking about whether we should have a

baby. We are really torn because we both travel with our jobs and someone would have to stay home and, quite frankly, neither one of us is having that burning desire. Also, based on all the information I've gathered from many of the mothers that I've spoken to about this, raising a child is the most demanding thing you will ever do—albeit rewarding, but very demanding. I can hardly keep up with the tasks of business and running a home as it is, let alone putting a child into the middle of all of this! I really don't know how the working mothers of the world manage to make it all work.

I also worry about raising a child in this day and age. How can you possibly protect them from all of the elements that are out there today? It doesn't seem like a child-friendly world out there to me. It's almost like anything goes.

But I think the thing that concerns us the most is the traveling and the time that Marco would be spending away from his child because I would probably be the one who would have the child with me the most. So we'll see. I'm going to give my mind and heart a rest for today and just not worry about it for now.

January 3rd

Well, we got up this morning and I'm so glad that it is still the holidays. Sometimes, you don't realize how hard you've been working until you stop, so I think I'm still recovering from a very busy November and December. The November and December period is usually a slower time for me when it comes to touring, but I did the Huron Carole Christmas tour this past year starting in Newfoundland and ending in Vancouver. This is a concert series that Tom Jackson has been running for sixteen years now. The proceeds go to needy families in each city that we play. In 2003, the bill included The Nylons, Beverly Mahood, and Brad Johner. I had such a great time, and the sound and lighting and crew guys were top of the line. It was a great Canadian show.

I also did my own Christmas tour in Ontario. It was the

first time that I've done this. I have always enjoyed Christmas, but I had never done a Christmas tour because I was still sorting out my faith in Christ. Once I chose to believe in what the Bible says about Christ, then I was able to stand on stage and sing about His birth and the sacrifice God made through his Son. I can't sing something on stage in front of all of you unless I believe in what I'm singing about. But now that I believe, I can't wait to do a Christmas tour again this year!

One of the things that Marco does to spoil me is make me hot tea and bring it to me in bed in the morning. We used to drink coffee, but we both did a ten-day fast and couldn't drink coffee. So we decided to stay off it, and now I drink tea.

The fast was a pretty amazing experience for me. Marco and his brother and sisters have been doing the fast throughout the years. During the ten days you only drink this lemon-syrup-water mixture. I had watched Marco do it and was pretty impressed with his discipline, so I decided that I wanted to do it as well. Marco wasn't sure if I could. Of course, that was even more of a motivator for me. Well, I did succeed and it was really empowering. You're not as hungry as you might think you'd be. My skin and my body felt clean and clear, and my energy level was much better. It's a good way to detox your body and I look forward to doing it again.

Anyhow, back to Marco bringing me tea in the morning. I really need the first half hour in the morning to just lay in bed and wake up slowly before I'm ready to deal with the world, so it's nice to start with a hot cup of tea. I always make sure there is a supply of Red Rose tea on hand, not only for myself, but for my many Canadian friends who also live in Nashville and grew up drinking Red Rose tea like I did.

After my tea, I'm ready to get after it. Just imagine what a baby would do to my need for a tranquil half hour in the morning! My mother didn't know what to do with me in the morning. I was the most difficult of the five kids to get out of bed. I missed the school bus a few times. Looking back, there were some pretty tense mornings because my mother would have to drive me to school and we lived out on the farm about ten miles away, so no wonder she was upset a time or two. She was a working mother. She would have to rearrange her schedule just to get me to school because I wouldn't get my butt out of bed. Sorry, Mom.

Today, we took down the Christmas decorations. It all came down easily. It always comes down faster than it goes up. We do it up pretty good around here, but I toured until December 22 this year, so it wasn't as extreme as in some years. But it's a must around here for Marco and me to have a winter wonderland in the house. But now that the decorations are taken down, we've moved it all upstairs and I just have to organize and put it away. It's a big job, but I enjoy it.

The Christmas season is special for Marco and me because he asked me to marry him on Christmas Day in 2001. We were watching *It's a Wonderful Life*, and we laughed and cried throughout the whole thing. (No matter how many times I've seen it, it still gets to me. I think that's partly due to the power of Jimmy Stewart's acting and certainly the message of how important family is.) I thought it was so great to see Marco reacting with his heart like he was. When it was over, I told him I would never be able to watch that movie with anyone else but him ever again. He turned to me and said, "Maybe you don't have to," and he got down on his knee and asked me to marry him. It was beautiful and it's a great memory for us.

I also like to cook traditional Polish food for Christmas. I am half Polish and the rest of me is French, Irish, and Indian. My mother is Polish and she taught me how to cook cabbage rolls, pierogies, borscht, etc., so we have quite the feast around here. I usually make enough so there are leftovers, and we share them with our friends. My mouth is watering as I'm writing this. Just another eleven months to go.

Football is a big event around this house. When the Titans are playing, we make every effort we can to watch. So we watched the Titans play tonight and they won. Pizza is usually on the menu. Double cheese, fresh tomatoes, and pineapple. Now keep in mind that sitting still for me is a bit challenging, so I will watch a little football, and then I'll do a little fussing around the house, and then I'll sit down and watch some more, and then I'll go to another TV and flip channels and so on. But I'm getting better. Some of our friends are serious football fans, and Marco is no exception, so we have some fun football parties.

Marco and me on our wedding day, April 20, 2002.
Photographer: Laura Rexroad

We went to church this morning. It's one of the things that I love to do with Marco. I find it really attractive that he is a man of God. A man on a spiritual journey. Our church is called BCC, which stands for Bellevue Community Church. The pastor is David Foster and he communicates the word of God in an everyday kind of way that I find easy to relate to. There are no rituals or anything like that. You just arrive, have a seat, and enjoy a good and empowering message from the Bible spoken in understandable language that relates to life and the joys and challenges we human beings have to deal with. It's really great to have a church like this to go to. I look forward to the Sundays that I can attend. It's non-denominational (though it is Christian), and I would certainly encourage anyone to check out the website at www.hopepark.com. You can hear the services online. That was my subtle way of putting a word in for God. How'd I do?

Watched some more football and then went to my manager's house this evening and had a fantastic salmon dinner. Hats off to the chef, Sue, Brian's wife. Sue is also my business manager and the three of us have been a team for nineteen years. That's really something: in the face of some very challenging times we still remain a thriving team. We've pretty much seen it all, together. People will often ask me how I've managed to survive in a business like this and I'm not sure if I would have without the support and hard work of Brian and Sue.

Their kids were also there: Kim and Kevin. I guess "kids" is the wrong word to use. I have watched them grow up. Kim has finished four years of university in Chicago and is now studying in Germany. Kevin is a really gifted drummer and I'm enjoying watching him grow into a young man.

Tonight is our last night of holidaying. Then it's back to doing what we do. I'm feeling inspired by the new year.

January 5th

The end of the holidays has arrived. It was so nice just for

Marco and me to have that time together. I guess I haven't explained what Marco does for a living yet. He sells a product called the Air Chair. It's the most comfortable thing I've ever sat in and it hangs from where ever you can imagine, but it is great for outdoors—under a tree, or porch, or patio. He also is developing another product that we're quite excited about, so I'll keep you updated. He travels around to a variety of home and garden shows. Fortunately, he is his own boss, so I can go out on the road with him sometimes, as he does with me. He can also put me to work out there with him, which I really appreciate because I like to hook up with him out on the road. But I have to make myself useful. I couldn't just go out and shop or hang out in the hotel room until he's done work. I also really enjoy it and it's quite different from what I do, although it is still working with people, which I enjoy. Marco is so good at dealing with people that I learn from him and enjoy watching him work.

Marco also plays guitar and spent a few years out there running the roads. It's nice to have another guitar player in the house—especially someone who knows what they're doing. Marco started out on classical guitar and taught for a few years as well, so if ever I have any question about a chord on the guitar, all I have to do is ask and he can show me. Sometimes when I'm writing, I don't always play the guitar. I'll just let the other writer play the guitar while I focus on lyrics or just singing the melody I'm hearing. We then try to find it on the guitar or piano. The only problem with that is then later I have to learn how to play the song, so I sometimes need Marco's help.

I'm also hoping that we will spend some time songwriting together. He's got a really witty mind and he's very funny, so I think it could result in some good songs.

You should check out Marco's website: www.airchair one.com.

We made it to the gym today and then I cleaned house and did laundry, paid some bills, and booked some songwriting appointments. I'm starting to write my new record with the hopes of getting into the studio sometime in April or May. I set up a lunch with Kyle Lehning, a producer I would like to work with. He ran Asylum Records for seven years here in Nashville and has produced all of Randy Travis's records as well as hits for Dan Seals, Bryan White, and many others. He is also considered "a good song guy," which means he has a good ear for a good song. I know what I want to do and what I like to sing about, so between the two of us we should have some fun together and make a great record. But we'll see what happens.

You are about to go through the process of making a new record with me. Get ready, 'cause it's a roller coaster ride! I go through a lot of emotional ups and downs while making a record. It means a lot to me that I do the best work I can. I dig deep and give all I have and then let it go and let the cards fall where they may. You see, after I'm done the record, the next step is to send a single to radio stations, and then they decide if they want to play it. If they decide to play it, you all get to hear it. If they decide not to play it, then you don't get to hear it, and I don't get to know how you feel about it. That's just how it works. There are a lot of artists releasing songs every week. You just have to hope your song will be played and there will be a reaction from the listener. So here we go.

We went to the movies tonight and saw *The Last Samurai* with Tom Cruise. It was really good and I didn't eat any movie popcorn or candy or anything. How long have I been keeping this New Year's resolution? Only five days. Oh, give me strength!

My mom and sister had a little disagreement during the Christmas holidays and I'm trying to stay out of it. I'm the one in the family who tries to fix everything. I hope they talk things out. I wear my emotions on my sleeve. If you want to know how I'm feeling, all you have to do is ask. But get ready, because I'll tell you. I seem to feel things really deeply and I have to talk about my feelings. Thank God, Marco is such a good and compassionate listener. I really need that. I remember his mother telling me that during a difficult time in her life, Marco was about seventeen and he would always come straight home from school and just be there for her so that she didn't have to be alone. How sweet is that? Families can sometimes be so complicated—especially between mothers and daughters. I like the saying "Seek first to understand and then to be understood." I know that when my friends or family take the time to try to understand how I'm feeling and maybe everyone takes some responsibility for what's going on that the problem can often be resolved, but you have to be willing to talk. I'm not holding my breath that these two are in any hurry to talk. They, unlike me, are not so quick to reveal their true feelings. I guess I got all those genes. The good thing about that is that I don't have a lot of unresolved issues. I like to communicate.

January 6th

Went to the gym. Wrote with Patricia Conroy and Lisa Brokop. I like the song, but it's hard to be objective. I'm really hard on songs, particularly my own, so we'll see how it turns out. I'm learning that if I'm not loving something, I still have to give it a chance. I had a meeting this afternoon with Brian, my manager, and Brad Burkett, my sound engineer and road manager. It's time to sum up last year and start making plans for this year. It was a good year and we're looking forward to doing it all again. We set goals for the year and then review at the end of the year and see how we did. An example of that is we try to set time lines for when we want to get into the studio, when we want to have the first single out, how many dates I want to be on the road touring, etc. It's always great to review and see what we achieved and what we did not achieve and what we could have done differently or better. I think it helps to keep you on track. This is where it is good to have the kind of manager that I have because he helps to keep me on track and focused.

Marco and I went out for dinner tonight to a Japanese restaurant called Omikoshi. It was so good and fresh. This is the type of restaurant where the chef cooks the food right in front of you. We enjoy the whole process.

It's late and I'm going to go to sleep now. Believe it or not, we sleep with our dog and our two cats. Everyone has their spot and it's so cozy. Our cat Marge likes to sleep on my left-hand side under the blankets as close to me as she can. Gracie, our dog, likes to try to sleep between us, but we try to keep her at the foot of the bed. Our other cat Caesar waits until everyone else is settled in and tries to sleep on Gracie's head. Gracie puts up with that for a little while, and then usually there's a little fussing that goes on until everyone is settled and Marco and Gracie start snoring and all is well. Everyone is piled in, so I'm going to shut off the light now. Goodnight.

Our family: Gracie and Marge on the sofa, and Caesar behind them.

Marco left this morning for Oklahoma. He'll be with family because he has a sister that lives close to where he's doing the show, so he can stay with them instead of in a hotel room. I was going to go with him so I could get some family time as well, but I really need to stay here and focus on songwriting. I love his family and I would have enjoyed the visit.

I remember the first time I met Marco's family; I was so comfortable and felt like I belonged, like I was a member of the family. That was a good sign for me as far as my feelings about making this permanent with Marco were concerned.

If this home show was only a few days, that would be all right, but it's ten days long, and it's a ten-hour drive. We would want to travel together, but I don't want to be gone for ten days right now. I really need to stay put.

Brian and I had dinner with Kyle tonight. We continue to talk and see if we are on the same page. It's important to me that we make a record with great songs that has a uniqueness about it. I don't want to do the same old, same old. I want each of my records to offer something a little different. Kyle feels that my voice is where the uniqueness starts and that using the lower register of my voice is really important, and I agree. I also like to find or write songs that make me feel something when I hear them. That may mean joy or sadness but goose bumps are always a good sign. I want this to be a record I can be really proud of.

Now all that being said, it's important for an artist to find a producer who can help them create the record that they have imagined and I think that Kyle will be able to help me achieve that and to keep everything in perspective. We are courting each other right now, so to speak. I know that Kyle needs to be excited about the artists whom he's working with, so he is also checking me out. We'll see what happens. I believe that if we are supposed to do a record together, then we will.

Well, today has been a good day, except I didn't make it to the gym again. I'm not making excuses, but I decided to prioritize some things that I needed to do today. I got up and listened to the songs that are being considered for the record. There is one in particular that I really love. It's called "The Faithless Kind," written by a friend of mine, Michael Smotherman. He's a soul man. The way he wrote the song feels so honest to me. I hope I can sing it. We have to do some pre-recording work. Sometimes I can love a song, but it wasn't meant for me to sing and I've got to find that out. I do a guitar or piano vocal of the song. That lets me know if I should sing it or not. It's not always necessary, but sometimes it is.

I worked on some song ideas. I've got a variety of songs that aren't finished so I have to spend some time deciding whether I should finish them or not. There is a school of thought that you should finish every song you start. I struggle with that because there are some songs that I just don't want to finish.

I'm going to a Chicks with Hits meeting tomorrow and I'm going to sing and play guitar for the songpluggers at the meeting. I want them to hear some of the songs that I'm writing, and I want them to hear my voice just bare bones. Chicks with Hits is a group of girls who work for the publishing companies here in Nashville. Publishing companies sign songwriters to songwriting deals and then they try to get their material recorded. The Chicks with Hits girls will all gather with one of us artists in a conference room at one of the publisher's offices and play songs written by their songwriters. I will sit there and listen and decide whether I would like a copy of one song or another to consider for my record project. Then they put together a compilation of the songs that I liked, and a few days later it will arrive in the mail and I will sit and listen again and determine whether there is anything there that interests me. If there is, I will call in and put the songs that I like on hold. In other words, when a song is put on hold, they are not supposed play it for anyone else. These meetings are called pitch meetings and it's a lot of fun to hang with the girls.

Marco and I are thinking about getting a puppy. A child or a puppy? Hmm, a puppy sounds easier.

January 9th

I wrote with Patricia Conroy and Lisa Brokop. We sure do have a good time together and they're very talented girls. We're working on a song called "Ain't Rio Grande." It's about a guy named Rio and it's silly but cute, and has a fun chorus, so we'll see how it turns out.

The Chicks with Hits meeting went well, but I still don't feel like I've found the song yet.

Went out to dinner with Janie West. She is a songplugger (she pitches songs to artists and record labels) and is a member of Chicks with Hits. Janie has been a good friend. She suggested I call Kyle when I told her I was looking for a producer for my new album. She brings me good songs and she helps to keep me motivated and focused. It's important to have friends like that to talk to when you're feeling excited about a song or frustrated and concerned that the songs aren't coming.

When I got home tonight and got the mail, there was a guitar vocal demo of a song that I wrote with Paul Overstreet called "She's a Keeper." I think it's a good song. It's about a woman turning forty who is concerned that she hasn't met the man she wants to marry. I am finding a lot of people struggling with that decision, and I can relate to that. I was thirty-nine when I met Marco, and forty when I married him, because up until that point, I always had these questions about whether the person I was dating was the person I should marry. I dated some very nice guys, but until Marco, marriage just didn't seem like the right choice. I'm sure glad I waited, because I couldn't be happier. I hesitate to talk about how great my marriage is, because I also know how fragile relationships can be, but I've made a decision in writing these journals to be as open as I can and to share with you the good days and the not so good days. Today is a good day.

January 10th

Cleaned house, organized upstairs attic. That was a big job, but it always feels good to have things back in place. I could hire someone to help me with some of these tasks, but our home is our private place, and I'm not comfortable with the idea of having someone else going through all our stuff. I've always managed pretty well on my own. The Titans lost tonight, so that means that they didn't make it to the Super Bowl. That's a drag. Oh well, there is always next year.

January 11th

Went to church and then to lunch with a group of my friends from the church. I was surprised to find out how many of my friends go to the Bellevue Community Church. Then I came home and finished up some house cleaning. It's nice to start the week with a clean house. I do like to have things clean and organized, but I'm not as obsessive as I used to be. Since I've met Marco, I spend more time doing fun things like watching movies and hanging with friends and less time obsessing about having everything in order. It's been good for me, but it took some time—although there does have to be a certain degree of order before I can relax. I'm not very good at sitting around in a mess. My family members always enjoy it when I come to visit because I like to be helpful. I do seem to have the ability to look at a mess and organize it effectively. My sister, Lori, has two children—my niece, Bryanna, and my nephew, Cody—and she and her husband, Ed, have started their own business, so, needless to say, she has her hands full and I get a chuckle when I get a phone call that goes something like this: "Sis, it's time for a visit. Help!" I need to organize a visit. I miss them.

My sister Lori, brother-in-law Ed Alexander, niece Bryanna, and nephew Cody.

January 12th

Went to the gym and set up songwriting appointments with Carolyn Dawn Johnson, Patricia Conroy and Lisa Brokop. I went to the doctor for my annual check up. All is well, although I do have to get a mammogram. I've done it once before and it wasn't as bad as I thought it would be, but I'm still not looking forward to it. But it's important that I take care of myself. Girls, we have to do this. Ouch! Can't they come up with a better way?

January 13th

I wrote with Eddie Schwartz today. I want to write about the fact that we are all dealing with many of the same things in life. Whether it be keeping our relationships strong, maintaining our self-discipline, or just trying to stay on top of things. So we'll see if we can communicate that in a song. The idea is that there is a thread that runs between us and I hope that comforts you.

Eddie is a Canadian and had his own recording career. He has also had a great deal of success as a songwriter. One of his big hits is the song he wrote for Pat Benatar called "Hit Me With Your Best Shot." When I was about nineteen, I often went to a rock club in Chatham (where I was born, although I was raised in Merlin, Ontario). Anyhow, I used to go to this club on jam night and sing that song, so it's cool for me to get a chance to write with the guy who wrote it. And the fact that he's Canadian is even cooler. He's got a lot of experience, so it'll be interesting to see what we come up with.

I had my eyes tested this afternoon. They haven't gotten any worse, but I do need to get glasses, mostly for driving and for seeing across long distances. In other words, I have a slight case of nearsightedness. I had glasses a couple of years ago, but I lost them and it's taken me this long to get another pair. I went and looked at some cool glasses. I'm going to have to have Marco come with me. He owns about fifteen pairs of glasses. He's got great taste in styles of glasses, so I'd like to have his opinion. We met up for dinner at the Royal Thai restaurant and we're going to look at glasses tomorrow before he leaves for Atlanta.

January 14th

Ordered some cool glasses this morning. I'm glad I brought Marco. He left for Atlanta today. I always feel a little sad when he leaves, but we're grateful for his business and how well it's doing. It's just a lot of work and a lot of travel. It's also a good thing that we are both as mature and independent as we are. We try not to put to much emotion into the times when we're apart. Although we certainly miss each other, we just try to look at the good side of it all. There's never a dull moment, and it's always great to be together again.

I wrote with Carolyn Dawn Johnson today. What a great talent she is! It was a pleasure. We started something good. We'll see what happens with it.

I'm doing a songwriter night at the church tomorrow, so I need to practice the songs I'm going to do. This is just a regular songwriter night. It's not Christian music, although you can play that if you wish. This church has fantastic music: many of the best songwriters in the world attend this church; the talent pool is endless. The thing about Nashville is that there are so many great songwriters here, so that if you want, you can get out every night of the week and hear a group of songwriters playing somewhere. I should probably do more songwriter nights. It's really good for me to do. You are certainly naked, so to speak, because it is just you and your guitar and a song that you wrote. I'd better go and practice and get some rest.

January 15th

I worked out this morning. It always feels so good to get that out of the way. I wrote with Lisa Brokop and Patricia Conroy on the song "Ain't Rio Grande" again. It's a good song, but I'm not sure if it's for me. I don't like to say ain't, but I decided to go with it because I do think it's a good song. Once again we girls had a great time together.

Girlfriends are so important to have. For so many years out on the road, I was the only girl, so it's been especially fun for me in these last few years to reconnect with the "Ya-Ya Sisterhood." That's from the title of a book that I highly recommend.

The songwriter showcase at the church went well tonight. Afterwards, we went to a jazz club and heard some good music and had a few laughs. I got up and sang "Bring It on Home to Me." I haven't done that one in awhile, but it was fun.

January 16th

Did some organizing of the filing cabinets. I like to keep everything on file for the year; then I move everything into a portable file, put it in the attic, and start with the new year in my desk filing cabinet. I am also going to organize Marco's files. He's working so much that I think it is something I can do to help him.

I made some more songwriting appointments with Patricia Conroy, Arnie Roman and Eric Silver. Eric and Arnie were very involved in my last album, *Shut Up and Kiss Me*. Eric produced five songs and co-wrote several songs with me, such as "I Surrender" and "I Will Be There." Arnie co-wrote "Broken" and "Thank You for Your Love" with me. I enjoy working with these guys and appreciate them sharing their talent with me.

I sent Kyle a detailed e-mail about what I've been up to and what I hope to achieve with this album. I know that he is trying to free up time in April. He is working on Restless Heart's new album as well as Randy Travis's next project, so he's a busy man.

I want to have new music out as soon as I can, but one thing I have learned is that patience is really important, because you have to find or write the songs first and that has to be the main focus. It's important that I record songs I'm passionate about because I'm the one who has to sing them night after night. So they really have to be right for me. Easier said than done, but this is an area I won't compromise on. That's not to say that I haven't compromised on songs in the past, but I'm less inclined to do that now.

What often happens in country music is that the record label and the artist may have a difference of opinion on a song. If the record label really loves a song and believes that it's a hit, the artist may want to consider recording it—especially if there is a song that the artist really loves but that the record label is not that sweet on. There is a process of give-and-take to some degree. An example of that for me would be "He Would Be Sixteen." I have never been pregnant, and so I could not quite relate to the idea of giving a child up for adoption. So I played the song live to a few audiences and asked whether this was a song that they wanted to hear on the radio. The reaction was overwhelmingly positive. I started getting letters right away from people sharing their own stories. Needless to say, I recorded it. It was a great success for me; it really touched a lot of people. The power of a song is certainly what motivates me.

I had wanted to record "Walk Away Joe," the big hit for Trisha Yearwood, which she did as a duet with Don Henley of the Eagles, but I lost that battle...so you just never know. But I try to follow my heart and fight the good fight.

I ate chips and ice cream tonight and didn't make it to the gym. This was definitely a cheat day. Which we're allowed, right? Oh well, tomorrow's another day.

January 17th

Finished putting files in the filing cabinets upstairs and booked a songwriting appointment with a young writer named Noah Gordon. He is signed to Tim McGraw's management company, RPM Management, and is hoping to have his own record out sometime soon. He is also a good songwriter, so I'm looking forward to meeting him and writing with him. We'll see how it goes.

I need to buy a CD burner. I want to put together a compilation of songs that I really like by other artists and get it to Kyle, so he can further understand where I'm coming from. I need to get that done.

Worked out on my treadmill. I find that if I don't get to the gym in the morning that I'm not likely to get there at all, so I am trying to make up for that by at least getting a few miles done on my treadmill. It's a nice thing to have. I turn on *Dr. Phil* or *Oprah* and away I go. I try to do at least one hour and sometimes two. My short attention span gets in the way sometimes and I have to really force myself.

There is just no easy way to keep our bodies in shape. You have to watch how many calories you're eating and make sure you work out. Why couldn't I have been one of those for whom it just comes naturally? I think most people think that it does just come naturally for me, but I have to work pretty hard at it, especially since I hit age forty. I was warned by a few women in my early thirties that it gets even tougher when you hit forty, and it appears that they were right. Well, I enjoy a good challenge, so here we go!

January 18th

Organized all the drawers in the master bedroom, bathroom, and closet. Moved all the furniture and got to all the dust bunnies. I put many things into bags for Goodwill as well as putting several things upstairs until I lose the fifteen pounds I've gained since I've been married. Marco and I have certainly been enjoying our time together.

Finished the laundry and took a bunch of cardboard boxes to the recycling centre. I didn't go to church today but I did spend some time reading the Bible and tonight I'm going to have a nice hot bath and jump into bed and watch TV. I love to watch TV, but it has to be something on channels like the Discovery Channel or National Geographic. I also like HGTV and, of course, *The Simpsons*. I'm a pretty serious channel flipper. I have an attention deficit problem, so I need a lot coming at me just to keep me interested. When I look back on my school years, I was so hyperactive. My poor teachers and mother. I was pretty hard to control. Marco and I have decided not to have children, so she doesn't even get to have her revenge by me having my own hyperactive child. Sorry, Mom. At this time in our lives we are just not having that burning desire to have children. It seems like our lives are on full throttle all the time and I know that a child requires full attention. It's just not the right thing for us to do. (I think I just heard a sigh of relief coming from my band members—no screaming baby on the bus. I'm sort of kidding because I know that we would figure it all out and the boys in the band would be great, but...) We are certainly open to adoption some day. Our good friends Jimmy and Claudia Olander adopted a beautiful baby boy. He's such a great kid. Jimmy and Claudia, by the way, were mutual friends of mine and Marco's and they introduced us.

Got up at 4:30 a.m. and finished up all my paperwork and bill paying. I have most things paid by automatic draft from our joint account, but I need to get a few more things put on that system.

I wrote with Noah Gordon today. It was great. He brings a lot of energy and is very open with his feelings, his heart, and his life experiences. That for me is a key to writing. Getting to the heart of the matter and opening yourself up. I told Noah that I'm hoping to write something that is different from the same old same old (which is hard to put your finger on), so he said, "O.K., how about a song called 'Different.'" I thought that was funny, so we wrote a song called "Different." It's about a girl who has fallen in love and it's different than what she thought it would be, so much more than she thought it could be, and so on. It's good and positive. I look forward to finishing it.

As I'm writing this, I'm on a plane on my way to Ottawa to participate in a sponsorship drive for World Vision. Getting involved with this international child sponsorship organization has been such a great thing for me. I try to present an opportunity at my shows for people to learn about World Vision (and sponsor a child if they want to as well). I pray that we get a lot of kids sponsored tomorrow night. The reality is grim for so many of the world's children: starvation, disease, and little or no education. But through World Vision's child sponsorship program we can make such a difference in a child's life by providing food, health care, schooling, and hope. I had an opportunity to go to Zambia in 2002 and see firsthand the African people's desperate need. And I witnessed some of the wonderful work that World Vision is doing there. The experience changed my life. My website has pictures and journals of my African trip. Check it out. I think it's pretty interesting: www.Michelle-Wright.com.

Oh, I have finally arrived at my hotel room in Ottawa. It's been a long day, but a good one, and I'm tired. I'm going to practice my songs for tomorrow and then call it a day.

January 20ᵗʰ

The World Vision child sponsorship drive went really well tonight. It was very cold out, so I was happy to see so many people leave the comfort of their warm homes to join us. Some people came to find out what World Vision is all about, and some people came to sponsor more children. It was encouraging to see how many people sponsor more than one child. There are a lot of giving people out there and it gives me hope. I sang a few songs and spoke about my own experience in Africa. I'm always surprised at how emotional I get. It just seems to come out of nowhere. My memories are still very strong, but, once again, it was a life-changing experience for me and I wouldn't change any of the heartbreak for the greater good that it has created in my life.

I'm going to try to get a good night's sleep. I've got a morning flight and a border crossing, so I have to be at the Ottawa airport early. It takes me awhile to wind down sometimes, so I'm going to shut my brain off and watch some TV.

January 21ˢᵗ

I flew home today. Marco is home, too, and we had a fun evening hanging out. I cooked a nice meal. Some steamed vegetables and chicken and a delicious salad with some nuts and strawberries and fresh baked bread (from the store, of course, because for some reason I could never get my bread-maker to work).

I must confess that we are *American Idol* junkies. I wish we could get *Canadian Idol*. I don't understand why we don't get some Canadian channels down here. We get British channels, but no Canadian channels. Oh well. What can I do? We get pretty excited when we're watching these young people going after their dreams—especially when you know that

Photographer: Bill Borgwardt

someone really has what it takes and right before your eyes their dreams are starting to become a reality. I often agree with Simon. Marco says I'm pretty tough, but you gotta have the goods.

January 22nd

I wrote with Eric Silver today. It was good to see him. He

moved into a new home and it's really nice. We got caught up and wrote a song called "Wrong." I don't know how crazy I am about it. I try not to get in the way and just let the song be written, but sometimes I feel like I need to stop it and start something else. Just go in another direction. I'm struggling a bit. Some days are just better then others when it comes to song writing, but it seems like lately I'm not writing anything that is working for me. I've been here before and this too will pass.

Marco left for Memphis today. I miss him already.

I got to the gym. I'm so glad I got that done. That lifted my spirits. I'm going to have a quiet night and not worry about the challenges I'm having with writing and finding songs.

January 23rd

Kyle has officially come on board to produce my new record. I've never really worked with a producer who has credentials like his. I'm really happy about this.

I wrote with Eddie Schwartz again today. I'm struggling with forming a good, solid idea that's different or gives me that feeling of knowing I'm writing something special. I guess you can't do that every time. The problem is that I don't feel like I've done it yet for this record.

The good news is that we got thirty-five kids sponsored at the World Vision child sponsorship drive in Ottawa. Our goal was 1600 sponsors over the entire campaign. I believe that they are close to reaching that goal and they are confident they will surpass it. This is a very rewarding cause for me to be involved in. It makes me feel like I'm doing something useful with my success.

A bunch of us went out tonight to see Raul Malo, the lead singer of the Mavericks. He is of Spanish descent and has a band that he plays in besides the Mavericks that does cover tunes, particularly ones with a Latin flavor. From the moment the music started, people were dancing and up on their chairs.

It was really fun. It was great to hang with the girls without the pressure of songwriting.

January 24th

I stayed home and listened to songs that have been pitched to me to consider recording. I am also listening to a variety of songs that I like by other artists, so that I can put together a CD of songs for Kyle, so he can further understand where I'm coming from. I'm not wanting to copy anyone else—that's actually the farthest thing from my mind—but I am definitely inspired by other artists and I want Kyle to know the quality of songs that I'm looking for or trying to write. I enjoy Keith Urban, Patty Loveless, Norah Jones, Shania Twain, India Arie, Annie Lennox, just to name a few, so I'm including some of their songs on the CD. I'm enjoying listening to other artists' music—I find it inspiring. Sometimes you get so consumed with your own project that it's nice to take a break and step away for even a few hours.

January 25th

Went to church and then out to lunch. It's one of the things I look forward to. Went grocery shopping and had a quiet Sunday. Marco will be coming home from Memphis in the early morning. I miss him and look forward to him coming home.

January 26th

I wrote with Naoise Sheridan today, another fellow Canadian. It was a bit of a challenge for both of us. Naoise has the same standards as I have. He co-wrote the big hit "Young" for Kenny Chesney. You just have to keep working through it. We worked on something all morning. It wasn't really coming together, so we went for lunch and came back and worked some more. But still nothing happened, so we decided to book another day. Then Naoise suggested that before we call it a day, we should try to write something in half an hour, whether we loved it or not. Just write, without thinking about whether it is any good or not. Somehow the idea of "As Good As Gone" came up. There is absolutely nothing original about this idea. It's been written many times, but we just went with it. The song started out slow but ended up being up-tempo. We just blurted ideas out. Now it does say some things that I don't like to say, like, "Hey, you loser, you better get it together or I'm out of here." But it is a fun and sassy song.

So there you have it. Wrote a song in half an hour. It's not likely to win Song of the Year, but we had some fun with it.

Marco and I went for dinner at Jimmy and Claudia's. She prepared a beautiful meal and we had a great time. They have an old English Mastiff. His name is Thor and he is huge. It's like having a small horse in your house, but he's so cute and I really enjoy seeing him and our dog Gracie playing around. We met him when he was just a little puppy. Now he's about 120 pounds and apparently going to weigh 200 pounds when he's fully grown. Wow! They had another Mastiff before Thor named Elvis and he was sweet as well. We're dog people.

Marco and I consider ourselves very fortunate to have the friends that we have. We wish we could spend more time with them. Summertime is always great for that. We like to have our friends over and barbecue and spend time together. That's just a few months away. By late March or early April, the grilling begins.

January 27th

I stayed home today and slept in. Marco and I spent the day together. We went to an afternoon movie. We saw *Cold Mountain*. We enjoyed it. Marco likes to go to afternoon movies. We then went out to dinner at Carrabbas. It's an Italian restaurant that we frequent and a usual meeting place for birthday parties and such with our friends. It was so nice. We have to make time for each other. It seems like we are working all the time. Marco works most weekends, so we have decided that we are going to have to make Monday or Tuesday our day together or else we will hardly ever have down time. It's so renewing to have that time together. It's been a nice day and we're happy. Goodnight.

January 28th

I wrote with Noah Gordon today. We almost finished our song "Different." It's coming along nicely. I don't think that it's the song that I'm looking for as far as my first single, but it's a good song. What I need are the two great songs that I'm then going to build the record around. I don't have them yet, but I'll just keep writing 'cause you never know when you might catch lightning in a bottle.

I spent some time on the phone dealing with household things and helped with a delivery for Marco's Air Chairs. It's a good thing I'm a strong woman because I can move all those things around and take care of business if Marco needs me to. As much as he tries to do it all, he just can't, and he needs my help sometimes. I'm happy to do it. We make a good team.

We sponsor a girl named Miriam whom I met when I went to Africa. We sent some extra money to her on top of the sponsorship. That will allow her to buy some things for her four brothers and sisters. She sent us a picture to show us what she bought for the family home—mattresses, blankets, food, lantern oil, clothes, books, etc. I'm so glad we can help them. I know they are doing well and they are being taken care of. We keep regular contact and if she or the kids need anything we are there for them. They have their way of life and they don't need to be taken out of their villages and brought to some strange place. They just need help with the basics in life and, in turn, they can be productive members of their village and maybe help others. Of course, the problem is that many of the adults are dying from AIDS and leaving the children behind to fend for themselves. That is the case with Miriam. Thank God for World Vision because I don't know what would happen to her otherwise. It feels good to know that this is one way we can help and that it makes a world of difference to her. I've heard some people say the problem is too big to overcome. Well, I can assure you that Miriam is grateful that someone is helping her, and that she and her siblings are going to survive. When I met them they were all so sweet and they just wanted to be able to feed themselves and go to school. How simple is that? Miriam's story is on my website. You just have to go to my journals from Africa.

January 29th

I was going to write with Noah today, but he had to cancel because his little girl is sick. I went to the gym and then bought a CD burner and tried to figure out how to use it. I can't believe how technology can cause hours of aggravation. I have sent an e-mail off to technical support for my burner so they can walk me through it.

Marco left for Atlanta this morning. I am going to go grocery shopping and make some fresh salad and soup so that I have healthy food ready to eat. I just want to eat light for the next few days. I'm doing OK with my program, but it's still very challenging. I've lost a couple of pounds. I find that if I have healthy, prepared food I will eat better. But don't bring that ice cream into this house! My capacity to consume ice cream is potentially award winning.

It's been busy, so I'm looking forward to a quiet night tonight.

January 30th

I wrote with Patricia today. I'm so glad it's Friday.

January 31st

I cleaned house today. I love to have a whole day to just clean. The thing I like about cleaning is that if you just stay focused, when you're done you're going to have a sparkling, clean house. Not like songwriting. If I get up today to write a song, there is no guarantee that I'm going to have a song at the end of the day, or at least a song that's worth anything. I've got a bad attitude right now. I'm just going to have a quiet weekend by myself.

February 1st

Went to church and worked around the house while the Super Bowl game was on. I like to turn on the TV when I'm doing things around the house. I was invited to a couple of Super Bowl parties but I just want to lay low. I wish Marco was here so we could watch the game together, but he's working. Oh well. Watching football is just not as much fun when he's not here; if it wasn't the Super Bowl, I wouldn't be watching. I have HGTV on or something like it while I work around the house. I bet him that New England was going to win. Of course, that was just a guess because I really don't know that much about what's going on. But I'm happy to say that I won. I went to bed early tonight in order to do some reading. I have a couple of books to get through. I think I'll read Naomi Judd's new book. It's called *Naomi's Breakthrough Guide*.

February 2nd

Wrote a pretty good song with Steve Fox and Patricia Conroy today. I'm excited about it. There's an emotion and a melody with this song that I really respond to. I get goose bumps. That's such a relief because I haven't been feeling that way lately.

Steve came to the writing session with a great idea (and about half the song already written), and we just worked with it until it all made sense. It's called "Starting Over Again." It's sad because it's about the end of a relationship—but that's life isn't it?—and life is what I try to write about.

Sometimes, if the song is done right and the melody is good, it can be a song that you just want to hear over and over again, even if there isn't a happy ending. It's rare when that happens, but I feel like we've done that with this song. Patty Loveless and Alison Kraus do that well.

The story behind the song is true. It's about a woman whose desire in life was to fall in love with a good man, get married, and raise a family. But she had pretty bad luck when it came to her choices—even staying in an abusive relationship. I guess a few of us have been there. For me it was several years ago, but I'll save that for the biography (or maybe I'll share that at some point during these journals). She finally got out of that relationship and met this very nice guy. All the family thought he was great; they were so excited the couple were going to get married. They had the beautiful wedding, moved into a new house. One morning, about a year into the marriage, they were laughing and joking and snapping towels at each other and talking about the future and about having children. Well, that afternoon after work he came home and asked for a divorce. It totally floored her because she just didn't see that coming. That was it; it was over. Ten days later, the house was up for sale and she had moved into an apartment. She's really not sure what happened, but maybe it was the thought of having children and the fear of that further commitment. The really interesting thing about this girl is that she has found forgiveness and is grateful that he found the courage to do what he had to do before children came along.

I have three other songs that I've co-written that I'm feeling pretty good about. One is called "In the Blink of an Eye," co-written with Patricia Conroy and Gerald O'Brien. Gerald is also a Canadian who co-wrote "Still No Shangri-La" on my last album and he also co-wrote Amanda Marshall's breakthrough single "Birmingham." Gerald and I started the song. We had written some of the melody and a few words, but were having a hard time coming up with an idea that seemed worth writing about, so I asked Patricia to join us. We played her what we had so far and she had the idea for "In the Blink of an Eye," and the moment she said it I knew I wanted to write it. This song is about the fact that everything can change in the blink of an eye. Not unlike the story in "Starting Over Again," but this song is much more positive. It's about the fact that we all have some rainy days that we have to get through, but hold on because things are going to change. If there is one thing that we can count on, it is that change is inevitable. I like this idea because I do want this record to be inspiring.

The second song that I'm feeling pretty good about is the song I wrote with Paul Overstreet called "She's A Keeper," which I mentioned earlier. Patricia and I have also written a song with a writer/artist named Mike Reid, who co-wrote one of my favorite songs of all time, "I Can't Make You Love Me," which was a big hit for Bonnie Raitt. Our song is called "My Love Goes with You." It's a pretty good song about what a parent may say to a child as they are leaving the nest and taking on life.

There is another song that I co-wrote with Naoise Sheridan. It's called "When Somethin's Right." It's a feel-good groove thing. We'll see what ends up making it in the long haul. I'll just get up tomorrow and put one foot in front of the other and write again. I need to make a list of the songs that are in contention.

SONGS I'VE WRITTEN:
1. "In the Blink of an Eye"
2. "Starting Over Again"
3. "She's a Keeper"
4. "My Love Goes with You"
5. "When Somethin's Right"

OUTSIDE SONGS:
1. "The Faithless Kind"
2. "Like an Angel"
3. "I Give My Heart to You"

February 3rd

I was supposed to write with Eric today, but he had to cancel. I went to the gym instead and then spent time figuring out how to use my CD burner—and I'm happy to announce success! What's a little frustrating is that I was on the right track in the first place, but I second-guessed myself and thought I needed help and got taken down a few wrong roads, but now I'm back and getting the job done. I'm enjoying stepping out of my own world and listening to other artists' records. I've been pretty consumed with the making of my own record, so it's good to take a break.

February 4th

Marco left for Cleveland today. It's a long trip. He'll be gone for two weeks. But I'm going to join him halfway through.

I went to the gym and then wrote with Eddie and Patricia. I'm not crazy about the song we started. I like the music, but I don't like the lyrics. I'm starting to feel like I'm pissing off all the songwriters I'm working with because I keep rejecting what we're doing as not special enough, but then when we talk about it everyone seems to understand that the pressure's on to come up with songs that will make people sit up and take notice. Every artist faces this reality when making a record. When you hear that it takes a year or two to put a record together and that an artist may listen to several hundred and sometimes thousands of songs to find the ones that work for them, it's true. It's like looking for a needle in a haystack, so to speak. So we'll carry on and I'll try not to get discouraged. It's just that some days I feel like I have nothing to say. Maybe I need to take a break.

February 5th

Wrote with Patricia and Arnie; we stared at the walls. That happens sometimes. We just couldn't come up with anything that seemed interesting. The challenge is that I could write a song every day. You write a couple of verses, a chorus, a solo, another verse, repeat the chorus, and there you have it! But how many of those kinds of songs are going to end up in the "A" pile? I don't know.

I met Arnie while he was living in New York. One time I spent a whole week there writing. We just struggled and struggled trying to find some good up-tempo ideas, but we couldn't seem to come up with anything I thought was particularly interesting. Then the next time I came to New York we wrote two songs that made my last record, so there you have it.

Arnie is actually a brilliant songwriter, so it was good for me to see that he also struggles. It just reminds you that even some of the best songwriters out there have days like this. It was nice to see him again. He has moved to Nashville, so I look forward to writing more often with him.

February 6th

Wrote with Eric today. I then drove out to Hermitage, which is north of Nashville, to Steve Fox's house to do a guitar vocal demo of our song "Starting Over Again." I really like it.

Got home late from Steve's. I'm tired. Thank God it's Friday.

February 7th

I went to the gym this morning.

I want to redo the kitchen. We want it to have more of an Italian vibe, so I'm going to shop around today and start to conceive the design. My brother-in-law Pat is a fantastic artist: he's worked on the set design for a few videos, including videos for Lee Ann Womack and Norah Jones. So I'm going to ask him to help me—I couldn't be in better hands.

Shopping can be so tiring, so I'm going to put my feet up for the rest of the night and just relax and do some reading. I'm reading *The Da Vinci Code*. Marco got it for me for Christmas. It's a pretty good murder mystery.

February 8th

Went to church and my friends chose my house for the Grammy party tonight. One of our friends, Dinah, worked in the music business in L.A. for a few years and she had a tradition with her friends there to have a Grammy party every year, so she likes to do that with her friends here in Nashville. It was just the girls and it was a lot of fun. We enjoy cheering on our favorites. Everyone brings a dish of some kind and we overeat and have some laughs and talk about love and life.

February 9th

Wrote with Patricia and Eddie today. Recorded the guitar vocal demo with Noah for the song we wrote called "Different." It's a good song, but it's not great.

I have a song meeting with Kyle tomorrow. I'm going to play him some of the songs that I like and I'll see how he reacts. There's a lot of work to be done still and I know I haven't written or found the big hits yet. So I'm not anticipating that he's going to be over the moon about these songs although (like I wrote earlier) there are some pretty good songs. But in this competitive market, pretty good is not good enough. I've got to just keep the faith. I'm going to do a lot of listening tonight.

Tour dates are starting to come in. Typically this is a quieter time of year as far as touring goes. A lot of artists do what I'm doing and work on their upcoming albums during this time. In addition to my touring in Canada, I am doing a tour in America called the PaJAMa Party. The idea was conceived by Deborah Allen. The lineup is Deborah, the Kinleys (twin sisters), and myself. We are all on stage together from the start to the finish of the show and we sing harmony on each other's songs. It's great. These are really talented women, and it's such a pleasure to hang out and share a part of my life with them.

The only bummer is we've got a PaJAMa Party concert booked on the same day as my good friend's wedding. Mike

Basow is getting married, and Marco is going to stand up in his wedding party and I'm going to miss it! I was so looking forward to going to something that didn't involve me and just melting into the crowd. Oh well, that's just the way it is. Mike's pretty upset that I'm not going to be able to be there, but I can't put the rest of the PaJAMa Party out of work and he understands. But that doesn't make it any easier. Marco and I are going to take them out to dinner—just the four of us—and have some time together.

The PaJAMa Party: Heather Kinley, yours truly, Deborah Allen, and Jennifer Kinley.   Photographer: Raymond Hicks

February 10th

Did the demo at BMG this morning for the song I wrote with Naoise called "It's Just That Easy." It's a positive groove thing. I like it.

Wrote with Eric Silver today, but we just talked mostly. Sometimes you just have to hang out and talk. We're friends, so we share a lot with each other.

Then I had my music meeting with Kyle and, as expected, he feels like we have some good songs, but that we have to keep looking. He is also encouraging me to just relax and be confident that we will find them. I believe that also, but it does still cause me some restlessness in the meantime. I am hoping that I will be able to write the two starting songs that we're looking for, but he's encouraging me to stay open to the fact that I may find the songs from an outside writer. I didn't write at all on my earlier records and depended totally on the songwriting community. I just had to sit and listen to hundreds of songs until I found it. It's out there.

February 11th

Went to the gym. Finished up my CD compilation of some of my favorite songs by other artists, as well as the compilation of the songs I've written that I like. I will drop a copy off at Kyle's, as well as the manager's, on my way to Cleveland tomorrow.

I've got to pack for Cleveland tonight and make sure the animals are taken care of, as well as everything else, because I'm going to be gone for four days. The break will be good, although I am going to work with Marco, but it is a different kind of work. It's really hard because it's sales, but it's a nice change and I don't have to be in charge. Marco is. I really like working with him because we have a lot of fun and I feel like I'm sharing the responsibility for results with someone else.

One of the things that I like about Marco's business is that A plus B equals C. In other words, if you show up to work you are going to get some sales. Now that doesn't mean it's going to come easy. Lately, I feel like I've been showing up but coming home empty-handed. I just have to keep reminding myself that that's how it goes. It's been a couple of years since I've made an album, but I'm quickly being reminded of the task that lies ahead.

February 12th

Got up early and made sure everything is taken care of around the house. Dropped Gracie off at the kennel and dropped off the CD compilations at Kyle's and Brian's. The drive to Cleveland is about nine hours, so that will give me some time to go through more songs that have been pitched to me. Throughout the year, I receive a lot of songs and CDs from other artists as well as songwriters outside of the Nashville community, so this will be a good time for me to listen to all of that.

I enjoy jumping in the car and going for long drives. It was a pleasant drive and I'm glad to be here safe and sound with Marco. I'm tired. Goodnight.

February 13th

Worked very hard today. Working Marco's booth is at least a ten-hour day for me. He is usually on the job a couple of hours before I even get there, and when your head hits the pillow when you get back to your hotel room around 10:30 p.m., it's not hard to fall asleep. Today was a successful day.

We are staying in a suite with quite a nice kitchen. I am trying to have salad and chicken ready for us when we get back to the room. This is a challenging time to try and keep the diet going. I would have ordered pizza, and Marco always offers to take me out after work. But we're just too tired.

February 14th

I'm so glad I'm here with Marco! I'm glad I made the time to be here. It's Valentine's Day. When I arrived at the booth this morning, there were a dozen roses and a beautiful note written in a card waiting for me. I bought Marco a nice card and some chocolates; as usual, I managed to eat most of them. I always get so emotional when I'm standing there reading those cards at the store.

We finished work too late to go out for a Valentine's dinner. We're too tired to go out, anyhow. We'll wait until we get home. That's fine with me. As long as I'm here with him, that's what matters most to me. We had a great day.

I love Marco very much. He's just so right for me. I must confess that I almost missed the chance to be with someone so perfect for me. Marco and I met on January 11, 2001, at the Blue Bird Café, a legendary songwriter venue here in Nashville. I went over to say hi to my guitar player, Sean Smith, who was sitting with Jimmy and Claudia Olander and a few other friends. (Jimmy and I were both signed on with Arista Records, so we knew each other as well.) Jimmy introduced me to his friends, including Marco. The first time Marco looked up at me and smiled, something happened to me. I walked away from the table after just simply saying hi, wondering who he was. I found out later that all the people sitting around the table felt it as well. I'm not trying to over-romanticize our first meeting, but that's how it happened.

I came home that night continuing to wonder who he was, but I put him out of my mind because at this point in my life, after a few relationships, I was not exactly a romantic nor did I believe in love at first sight. I was lying in bed the next morning when the phone rang. I wondered if that might be Jimmy Olander calling me about that guy, but Jimmy's never called me in his life, so what was I thinking? Well, it was Jimmy calling me about that guy. He told me that Marco was intrigued by me. I responded by saying that I was intrigued by him, too, so they set up a dinner date for us to meet and hang out.

We had a lot of fun together, set up another date, and ended up dating for about three months. Marco was quite unlike anyone else I had ever met. He was sweet and kind and funny and a churchgoer and really loving towards me and he made me feel so good. Well now, I couldn't have that! Where's all the drama and uncertainty? There really wasn't any. It was just easy. Quite frankly, I didn't know how to deal with that. He wasn't the Bad Boy or Mr. Unavailable. He was just a straightforward nice guy. Marco is also a really funny guy and at first I thought that he was just too silly and too immature for me, so of course I had to break up with him.

We stayed apart for about ten weeks and he didn't call me or anything. He just left me alone. I really respected him for that and thought that that was best. But one day I asked my guitar player Sean to ask him something for me since they went to the gym together, and Marco later told me that he saw that as an opportunity to make sure that I was doing alright. So he sent a letter to me through Sean, asking me if I was OK. I was missing him a lot, but I thought that that was just part of the drama that comes along with all that breaking up and making up stuff. Still, I called him and we arranged a picnic the next day and the moment I saw him I just felt that warm good feeling that I always feel when I'm around him and I have never looked back. He's kept me laughing and feeling cared for and loved ever since.

He proved that I could depend on him and that he is a man of his word and his character is solid. So here we go. Say a prayer or two for us, would you? I hope we're going to beat the odds.

After writing this, I asked Marco what he thought of me when we first met (besides the obvious things that go on between two people who are attracted to each other). What he said was revealing. He said he thought that I was somebody who had been under the microscope for a long time, but he would get these glimpses of me when I would let down my guard and he loved what he saw. He knew that I had a big heart and just needed someone that I could love and count on. I had been Michelle Wright the singer, fighting the good fight for a long time, and I was very cautious. There wasn't a lot that I could depend on at this point in my life, whether it was when my next album was going to come out, or if the next single was going to be a hit, or would there be enough work on the books to keep everyone going, etc. So I thank God that He answered my prayers, because when I met Marco he was exactly what I was praying for, and we believe that God brought us together.

We had another great day today, but I'm so tired. Marco has better stamina than I do. I think I've met my match.

February 15th

Worked hard today. It's the end of the show. We tore down the booths and went back to the room and had pizza. Oh, how we love that pizza! We had record sales, and that gives us a great feeling.

I'm glad I can be helpful in Marco's business. Without me, he would have to bring along someone else to work for him, so I'm glad I can do it.

February 16th

Left early for home. Marco stayed to load up. I wanted to get home in time to pick up Gracie from the kennel so she doesn't have to spend another night there. My vet is the best, and they really love Gracie, but we hate the thought of her being in the kennel up the road when we're home. You have to pick her up before 6 p.m. or the doors are locked. She's just so happy to see us and we're so happy to see her! All you dog owners know what I'm talking about.

It always feels good to be home. I'd better get a good night's sleep because I'm back to writing again tomorrow. I hope the break was good for me.

February 17th

Wrote with Patricia and a new writer with whom Patricia suggested we write. Her name is Carol Mack Parker. The song is called "I Believe" and it's a pretty good song. I'm obviously writing a lot with Patricia. We're great friends and I enjoy writing with her.

Marco bought the DVDs for the series with Kiefer Sutherland called 24 and we're hooked. We stayed up late and watched several episodes.

February 18th

I wrote with Carolyn Dawn Johnson today. She was pretty tired. She has been on the road promoting her new single, "The Simple Life" (a huge task). And she just finished the video for the song in L.A. So it's all pretty grueling for her right now. We tried to finish the idea we started last month, but didn't feel like that was getting us anywhere, so we started another idea. I think they are both good ideas - we will have to get together again.

I came home and slept for a couple of hours. Woke up to Chinese food waiting for me. We're going to obsess and watch more *24* and eat Chinese food, so I've got to go.

February 19th

I wrote with a new writer today. His name is Mark Morton. I like him a lot. He's a great guitar player with a lot of soul. I like the idea we've started. It's called, "Where the Cool Water Runs." We'll see where it goes. It's definitely got a groove thing going on. It's pretty simple but it feels good.

Leftover Chinese food for dinner tonight. That's simple enough.

February 20th

I wrote with Patricia and Lisa today. We started to jump into something without really thinking about it, and I felt compelled to stop the process and make sure that we'd thought things through enough. I just didn't want to write another idea that didn't really do much for me. They're great friends and they heard me out and didn't think I was just being a bitch. I'm sure they did a little bit, but they understand what I'm trying to accomplish. They're both artists themselves. Lisa just finished an album that took two years to make.

That being said, Lisa and Patricia had written a great song called "Try Me Again around Midnight" a few weeks earlier. Not only is it well crafted, but it also has an honesty about it that I loved to hear. Lisa's record label and everyone involved with her new record thought the album was done, but they heard this song and went back into the studio to cut it. I can't wait to hear the studio version.

The reason I think Patricia and I make a good songwriting team is because she is free-flowing with her approach to songwriting, whereas I need to stop and think things through a bit more. The problem with my approach is that I will think myself right out of writing. So it's good for me to have someone who keeps the ideas flowing. Then I can grab on and take things to a place that works for me. But we do need to stop and allow me time to work on the ideas and see if we have taken the best advantage of them.

Today, after we stopped and thought things through for a few minutes and discussed a few approaches, we came up with an idea called "In the Absence of Love." I think it might be a spiritual song. A song about Jesus. All three of us girls are Christians and it's hard to explain (especially for me, since I am a relatively new Christian). I'd been on a spiritual journey for many years until I came to the conclusion that what the Bible says is where I would put my faith. I was baptized in July of 2001 at my childhood church in Chatham, Ontario, and since I've made this decision, so many things have changed in my life. Like the Bible says, God's love for us is eternal. I have found a peace in that, a serenity I can't quite explain, but I no longer feel the same kind of fear that I used to feel about whether I'm going to be successful or whether things are going to be okay. Without fail, in my life all things have happened the way they did because that's the way it needed to be. So I'm sure this record will have a certain spiritual slant to it as well. I hesitate to talk about my faith because, believe me, this does not mean that I'm some kind of an angel or sinless, but I have found what works for me. I can't wait to see *The Passion of the Christ*. I can only imagine how intense that is going to be.

I had a long conversation with Janie West today about my concerns in regards to finding songs. She has encouraged me to get out there and listen to more songs than just at the Chicks with Hits meetings, so on Monday I'm going to make appointments with a variety of publishing companies. I'll write in the morning and then listen to songs in the afternoon.

I had dinner this evening with two senior executives from TSC Stores in Canada, Roy Carter and John Kropp. TSC Stores is a Canadian-owned chain of stores in the province of Ontario similiar to the Tractor Supply Company outlets in the United States. Maybe you've seen the George Strait commercials for Tractor Supply in America? Well, I do similar work with TSC in Canada and I'm having lots of fun with it. Our dinner tonight was to celebrate the success of our relationship and its renewal for another year. I was raised on the farm and remember going to the TSC store in Chatham when I was a kid. Merlin, Ontario, where I was raised, is a small farming community about fourteen miles south of Chatham, with a population of around six hundred. The idea of a store that caters to the farmer is something I relate to and with which I'm proud to be associated. I also really like John and Roy and the other TSC staff members with whom I've worked, particularly John Couper. The owners are good, hardworking people who took a risk and bought out the previous ownership of the Canadian operation. Now the company is expanding and becoming a wonderful success story. So far, so good!

I'm involved with a number of things for TSC, but one of the things I do is participate in store openings. I'll show up at an opening to play some music, shake some hands, meet the people and sign autographs. I love it.

John and Roy even made me a pink leather tool belt and I use it because I'm the one around here who is the handy person. That's not necessarily Marco's strength (although he's open to learning). When you're raised on the farm you learn to do just about everything—from changing an alternator to fixing a leak in the roof. Whatever needs to be done. These skills have served me well.

Now speaking of autographs, when I'm on tour, I try to

sign autographs after my show whenever I can. But some-times I can't. For example, there are times that we have to leave right after a concert because the distance to our next show is too far. Or if it's too cold out, like at some of the out-door shows we play. I can't stay out there too long, so I may just have to sign my name without personalizing the auto-

Ready to work. Gracie's ready, too. I love my pink TSC tool belt.

graph. I know I've ticked a few people off by doing that, but if there's one thing I've learned, you can't please everyone and most people are understanding. I'm not being a wimp, but if I get sick that's just a drag for all of us. From the people who bought a ticket to those of us who were counting on the work.

I've only ever had to cancel one show, and that was in Winnipeg a couple of years ago. I had been booked to perform at a casino for two nights, but I developed laryngitis and totally lost my voice. Gone! The first night, I tried to get out on stage and sing. It sounded just awful and it really hurt, so I couldn't do the show. I couldn't have the paying audience sit through that! Everyone needed to be reimbursed, and I went to the emergency room right away. The doctor gave me a 10% chance of being able to sing the following night. He said the only way we might get better odds was if I took some steroids. The doctor warned me I might bloat out a little bit, but I decided I had to try the steroids and risk it. In fact, I ballooned about ten pounds right away! Now, girls, this is a nightmare. But I got through it, and sang the second night. We went back to Winnipeg a few months later and made up for the show we had to cancel. You don't want to have to go through that too often.

February 21st
_____

Cleaned house and celebrated the birthdays of two of my girlfriends, Dinah and Shelley. We went to Taste of India for dinner. It was delicious. I was the designated driver. On our way to the restaurant, we got into an interesting conversation about same-sex marriages. I have had conversations with people both gay and straight about this subject, and there certainly is a wide variety of viewpoints. What started the conversation is that two friends of ours, a gay couple, are going up to Toronto to get married, and one of the girls that was in the car is going up to be a witness. Personally, I think marriage should remain defined as a union between a man and a woman. Civil unions should be allowed for gay people, with the same rights as heterosexual unions. This is such a difficult issue for our society.

February 22nd

Went to church and laid low.

February 23rd

Wrote with Mark Morton today. We finished our song. I like it. It grooves along nicely. We're going to demo it at his home studio.

I'm a "resident alien" here in America. My green card was going to expire in a month, so I went and got it renewed. I had to go to the U.S. Immigration Office here in Nashville. They were very nice and everything went really well. A green card is good for ten years. Unless I change my citizenship, I will have to renew every ten years. I can't imagine changing my citizenship, so I hope it's always that easy.

Booked appointments to listen to songs.

February 24th

Had a cancellation, so I went to the gym and just did household tasks today. Doesn't it seem like it's just never done? I can't even imagine how you moms and dads out there are keeping up. We have a good-sized house, so it requires a lot of attention and, as you may have already figured out, I like things to be clean. The animals leave most of the mess it seems, particularly dog and cat hair. I just have to vacuum and dust every three or four days. But enough about that.

February 25th

Went to the gym.

Stopped by Universal Music Publishing and listened to some good songs. Cindy Forman—a girl who worked at a different publishing company in Nashville that closed its doors—is now working for Universal. There have been a lot of companies that have had to stop operating due to a downturn in the music business. Certainly, some of it has to do with downloading. It's been difficult to see many of my friends lose their jobs. Cindy landed on her feet, however. We've hung out throughout the years, so she's got a pretty good sense of who I am as a person and an artist. She played me some good songs. It was nice seeing her and I look forward to doing it again.

February 26th

Wrote with Patricia and Carol Mack Parker. We finished "I Believe." It's a good song.

I got my hair done today. It always feels so nice to get your hair done.

Came home and cooked a nice meal and worked on some of my journaling. I'm looking forward to a quiet night and some TV.

February 27th

Listened to songs at BMG. Michelle Berlin played me some good songs. Then I went to Wrensongs and heard some more good material. Ree Guyer played me some songs by singer/songwriter Sally Barris, and I really responded to her songwriting. Ree later introduced me to Sally and I'm going to write with her. I'm looking forward to that. I like her style.

Shopped for groceries and made dinner. I'm obviously the one who does the cooking around here and I really enjoy it. I cook and Marco does the dishes. That's a good arrangement, I think.

February 28th

Laid low. I mean really low. This was one of those days when I only got out of bed to get something to eat. I slept, watched TV, and slept some more. What a great day.

February 29th

Went to church. Took Gracie for a walk. Went for a drive in the country and Marco and I had our first official fight as a married couple. I called my sister and told her. She said,

"Good, now you're officially married." We're both just working too much and haven't been making time for us. We talked things through, and Marco put his arms around me—I felt so much better. He shows me love like that in spite of the fact he may still be a little miffed at me. I'm learning how to love by his example. Instead of being cold and distanced, he showed me love. How sappy is all of this? But as I'm writing this, I'm really appreciating how he loves me.

March 1st

Marco left this morning for Charlotte. I am going to join him on Thursday night. I had a listening meeting with Kathy Walker today. She is overseeing the song catalog of Randy Goodrum. I like his songwriting. She is also the sister of Michael McDonald, the great silver-haired singer from The Doobie Brothers. I didn't know this before I went to the meeting, but it was great to find that out because I'm a fan. She played me a few of his songs. We spent a couple of hours together and had lunch. It was a pleasant way to spend some time. Once again, I'm not sure if I heard anything that I really loved, but we'll see. I'll have to go in and listen some more.

March 2nd

Noah cancelled today. He's been really sick. Ended up with pneumonia, which landed him in the hospital. Everyone seems to be getting sick. But I somehow have managed to avoid a winter cold so far.

I went to the gym and spent time working on my journals. I'm a bit behind, but I guess that is to be expected. This reminds me a little bit of school and I was never really good at that. It's the whole routine thing. I've been journaling for myself for about seven years now—but that was just when I wanted to, not when I had to turn so many pages into a publisher. I have to turn in my journals every three months, and I'm hoping that what I'm writing is interesting enough. Some days are just pretty basic. I get up, write a song, come home, make dinner, watch some TV, and go to bed. Actually, right now a lot of days are like that. Oh well, I'll just do my best.

Once I start touring more, there may be more to talk about, but there is also a routine that occurs out there on the road. I'll just keep writing.

March 3ʳᵈ

Wrote with Colin Linden today. It was great. He's a nice guy. It's our first time writing together and I like the idea we've come up with. Colin is a blues musician/singer/song-writer. He brings a lot of experience with him. I grew up listening to a lot of Motown music and I really would like to find a way to incorporate a blues or an R & B feel into at least one of the songs on my new album. The song we started seems to have that vibe.

Colin co-wrote "Guitar Talk" for my *Now & Then* album. The song went to #1 on the country radio charts in Canada. He also played guitar on the *O Brother, Where Art Thou?* album. He appeared in part of the documentary on the making of the album, *Down From The Mountain*. And he's in a Coen brothers movie that was out recently called *Intolerable Cruelty*: he plays the priest who marries Catherine Zeta-Jones and Billy Bob Thornton. Colin obviously has a diverse musical background and has had success in the areas of the blues, country, and bluegrass, with a little acting thrown in for good measure.

We took a lunch break and met up with my band at Taste of India. I haven't seen the guys for a few weeks and they all know Colin, so it was a good visit.

March 4ᵗʰ

I had another cancellation today. I was actually glad because I am leaving for Charlotte today to hook up with Marco and there always seems to be so much to do before-hand. I cleaned house and packed, made sure the cats' sitter was organized. I had to pick up my car from the dealership—there were a bunch of things that had needed to be fixed.

Dropped Gracie off at the kennel and headed off to Charlotte.

I brought a bunch of songs to listen to on the way. I found a few good ones. Once again, Sally Barris' songs really stand out for me. I've got to call her and set up a writing appointment.

I arrived safely and, as always, it's nice to be here with my Marco.

March 5th

Marco and I got up and worked out. It always feels so good. Worked really hard at the booth and then went out for dinner. We had a good day.

March 6th

Worked hard and had another great day. Hooked up with a friend of ours, Bobby Short, and had a great dinner. We went to a Japanese restaurant, which happens to be one of his regular stops. Bobby's a single guy, so he eats out quite a bit. He works in the steel industry and spends a lot of time in Asia. During his travels, he's come across a few sushi combinations that he likes and the chefs at this particular restaurant make them for him.

I can't eat any type of raw fish, so I ate only the things that were cooked. It was nice to spend some time with Bobby. We haven't seen him in a couple of years. We got back to the hotel room too late in the evening, but sometimes you've just got to hang out and enjoy life.

March 7th

Another hard day's work. Tore the booth down and helped Marco load up the frames before I left on my own to come home because I have to write tomorrow. We got caught up in some pretty strong winds while loading up the frames. I found out that they were tornadoes while I was listening to the weather on the drive home.

I listened to all the songs that I brought with me, and I've found a few that I like. I need to make a compilation CD and get it out to Kyle.

It's 2 a.m. and I'm tired. I need to get some sleep. Tomorrow's another day.

March 8ᵗʰ

Slept in. Started laundry. Noah came over to write. We started a new song.

Mark Morton came over in the afternoon and we finished our song called "Where the Cool Water Runs." I thought we had finished the song earlier, but we decided to work a little bit more on it. I like where we ended up with it. It's pretty cool. We're going to do a guitar vocal demo at his place.

Marco got home around 5:30 p.m. and I had a nice dinner ready. Tuna steak, steamed vegetables, and yams. We don't do yams that often, usually just on Thanksgiving, but they sure are good! Brad Burkett, my road manager and sound engineer, barbeques a lot for us out on the road. He always uses his trusty cajun spice and since I really like it, I use it occasionally when cooking as well. I love to cook and Marco loves to eat. I know

I love to cook.

that he really likes it when he comes home off the road and there is a nice dinner ready. I enjoy doing that for him. I like to eat, too, so it's a fun way for us to spend time together. Unfortunately, it challenges the waistline, but oh well!

Marco loves to watch movies and now he is into buying DVDs of cable TV shows such as *The Sopranos* and *Six Feet Under*, and we are enjoying watching them. We've started to trade out seasons with a few of our friends, so there are phone calls coming in that sound like this: "We stayed up all night and finished the first season of such and such...we'll switch out the first season of such and such if you guys give us the second season of such and such..." You get my drift. A bunch of us are obsessing on this all at once. I think a friend of ours, Dave, started it. It's his fault.

March 9th

Worked out. So much laundry to do. When Marco comes home from a long trip there is always lots of laundry, but I like to do it for him if I can, although he is quite capable of doing it himself (and he does). We have a very traditional marriage in many ways, and that's the way we like it.

Finished "In the Absence of Love" with Patricia Conroy and Lisa Brokop today. The song did end up being about our faith. That's pretty cool. It's the first time I've written a song about Jesus.

Terri Clark is going to record one of Lisa's songs. Lisa also has a song on Reba McEntire's new album. That's great! We are also getting ready to do a demo of "Ain't Rio Grande."

March 10th

Marco left this morning for Birmingham. I'm going to join him tomorrow night.

Wrote with Patricia and Arnie today. The song is called "This Endless Night." I like it.

I've arranged to do a demo for "The Faithless Kind." I'm going to do it at Bob Funk's home studio. Bob is Patricia's fiancé and he does good work, so I'm going to try to do as much of my demo work there as I can.

Got all my tax information off to the business manager. It always feels good to have that done.

March 11th

The demo for "Where the Cool Water Runs" went well.

I'm packed and ready to go to Birmingham. I joined Marco there last year as well. While we were there, our van was broken into and both of our guitars were stolen. Eight thousand dollars worth of guitars. The loss was particularly tough for Marco. He used to live in L.A. and while he was there he waited tables while he studied acting and played music and so there was a lot of hard work that went into the purchase of that guitar. It also represented a certain time in his life that was special to him and that guitar was there through a lot of it. I have a sponsorship with Larrivee Guitars, a Canadian brand, so my guitar was relatively new. We were able to have both guitars replaced by Larrivee for a minimal fee. The company makes great guitars, so Marco and I are enjoying playing our Larrivees.

I have a guitar that carries a lot of memories for me. It was my first guitar that I brought out on the road. It is now in the Canadian Country Music Hall of Fame in Calgary, Alberta.

Yes, we do have a Hall of Fame in Canada, too, and it's really great. There is a lot of Canadian country music history represented there, from Hank Snow to Shania Twain. It's an honor to have a full exhibit in it.

My drive to Birmingham was nice. I found out today that we've got a show in Ottawa coming up soon, so I'm going to be able to arrange a visit with my sister, Lori, Ed, and the kids. My brother, Steve, is living with them right now as well because he started a new job in their area, so I'll get to see them all, and I just can't wait. Everyone's been pretty busy so we haven't had much family time lately. I'm really looking forward to it.

At the Canadian Country Music Hall of Fame.

March 12th

Worked hard as usual. We had another good day. It's a very unique discipline that is required when dealing with people all day long. It's a good thing Marco and I enjoy working with the public.

We like to go to the Outback Steakhouse when we're here. I'm trying to eat well, so I've been having coconut shrimps, mushrooms, and vegetables. I like how they do their mushrooms and the service is really good. The servers are very friendly. Marco and I have both waited tables at different times in our lives so we know it's not an easy job.

We're tired tonight and ready for a good night's sleep.

March 13th

Worked hard. Good day. It's fun to watch people check out the Air Chair and then see their reactions when they sit in it. It's so much more comfortable than you would think. It really surprises them. In many ways the Air Chair sells itself, but the art of salesmanship is still required and Marco is so good it's fun for me to watch him, too. He told me he likes it when I come out on the road with him, not only because it's so great to be together, but he also gets a lot of energy from me. These are twelve-hour days and it's nice to have someone to share it with. I just put my glasses on and tuck my hair in a cap. I rarely get recognized, but when I do, people get a kick out of it and I usually end up signing their chair. It's fun.

March 14ᵗʰ

Worked hard and had a good show. Tore down the booths and drove home. It's about a two-and-a-half-hour drive.

Gracie was here waiting for us. She's so cute. Whenever we're away, I always have one of the neighborhood boys get her out of the kennel if we're going to be home that night.

It's late and we're all in the bed and it's time to shut her down. I'm back to songwriting tomorrow.

Marco and Gracie.

March 15th

I wrote for the first time today with Britton Cameron, another one of Patricia's co-writing buddies. Patricia enjoys writing with Brit. I listened to some of the things they've written together, and I liked what I heard. I'm glad we got together. Brit brings a lot of energy and enthusiasm. We wrote a song called "You're My Meant-to-Be." I like it. I just picked up the guitar and started playing an up-tempo rhythm and we went with it. We had a good time and I look forward to us writing together again. It's always great when you finish a song in one day.

March 16th

Had a new air conditioner installed today. Stayed home and booked more songwriting and listening appointments. Household duties kept me busy all day.

March 17th

Marco left for Fairhope, Alabama, today. He will be staying with a friend that used to work with him in his band days back in L.A. They have been friends for a long time. His name is Rex Anderson and I love him, too. He's been a good friend to Marco.

This is a very busy time for Marco. It seems like he's gone a lot these days. When I was planning our wedding, it was during this time of year. I remember feeling like I was planning a wedding with someone that I was hardly seeing. But all I had to do was just see him for one day, and I knew I was doing the right thing.

I'm reminded right now of how busy a time of year this is for Marco. It does slow down in April, May, and June, however. So we look forward to that. It was important to me that I marry someone who was as hard of a worker as I am. I wanted a partner who took pride in what they did. I respect that. Obviously, Marco fits the bill. I was going to go with him to Fairhope, but I decided I needed stay home and work on my journals.

I'm also feeling a little under the weather. Marco has been sick and I think he may have passed it on to me. So many people are sick. I thought maybe I was going to avoid a cold, but the way I'm feeling right now I don't think I will. I think I'll take a nap and then work some more later tonight.

March 18th

I sure am glad I decided to stay home and work on my journals. It is a serious commitment and I have had some catching up to do. I have a three-layer system that works for me. I have a daily book in which I write my daily appointments, and then I have a journal book in which I jot down points that occur throughout the day. Then I develop everything into sentences and paragraphs for the journal's publisher. The end of this month will be my first submission.

I have to say that I'm challenged by trying to make my daily life sound more interesting, because it's pretty routine on some levels. I am doing a lot of writing, though. Between trying to write my next album and writing this book, it's pretty all-consuming. This writing requires a discipline that I haven't had to practice since school. But in certain ways, I'm enjoying the challenge.

I'm definitely coming down with a cold and I need more rest than usual. I hope this doesn't last too long. For some people I know, this virus is something that seems to be hanging around way too long. I'll get some rest and see how I feel later.

Marco is enjoying his time with Rex. Rex lives right on the water in Alabama, so Marco enjoys hanging out there after work instead of staying in a hotel.

March 19th

I woke up early this morning and just starting coughing. Before I knew it, I was in the fetal position, sweating and coughing. I fell back to sleep for a couple of hours, but I had to get up and go to a writing appointment with Gerald and Patricia.

We want to finish "In the Blink of an Eye." It needs to be shortened. It's four-and-a-half minutes long. That's OK if the song needs to be that long, but this one doesn't. It can be shortened. It's been hard to get an appointment together because we have all been pretty busy. Gerald has been hired to do some of the music for *Entertainment Tonight*, and he's been spending time in L.A. But today we came up with a better arrangement for the song, and talked about organizing a time to demo it and which musicians we want to use.

I was supposed to go with the girls tonight to a Bible study and concert, but I'm just too sick. I need to go to bed. Goodnight.

March 20th

Spring begins. This is my favorite time of year. But as I write this I know I really like all the seasons. It's time for me to get out in the yard and clean everything up and plant new things. I grow a vegetable garden every year. I'm going to plant fewer vegetables this year and try to pay more attention to them. I'm also going to put newspaper down and then mulch on top of the paper. Apparently, that's one of the best ways to keep the weeds away and how I try to keep my garden organic, and then I can just integrate or plow that stuff back into the ground at the end of the season. I grow tomatoes, basil, peppers, zucchini, dill, squash, beans, and I may try some new things this year. I'm not sure what, but we'll see.

We also have a very large deck that I like to put a lot of potted plants and flowering trees on. Marco wants to build a big trellis over the deck and grow grapevines on it. It's going to look great.

I'm still feeling a little under the weather, so I'm spending time working on my journals and laying low.

March 21st

Well, I got up feeling better and I went to church. The subject today was about making good use of your time and that time is a gift and we don't all have the same amount of time here on Earth. I know that everyone is dealing with a variety of things in their lives, but I try to appreciate every day as it comes. Now that doesn't mean that some days I don't just feel overwhelmed, and sometimes I have lower energy than other times, and sometimes I deal with a bit of depression (or at least I think it's depression because I don't feel like doing anything); but if I get a workout in and everything is flowing in my body, I feel better and I'm ready to get on with it.

The key is that you have to make the workout happen. I'm convinced that working out or getting some form of physical activity in your daily life is really important. I also believe that depression can be the result of a chemical imbalance; it just seems to me that if I get enough physical activity and my blood circulating, I feel better.

The service was also about how often we wish we were doing something else for a living, or wishing we were living somewhere else, or wishing we could be someone else, etc. The message was "try not to wish your days away." I guess we're all guilty of that to some degree. I am really grateful for everything in my life because things are really great for me. But it's not always that way, so I am enjoying the goodness in my life right now (although I am continually being challenged by my career, but who isn't?). I think it's important to find joy in what is in our lives and to continue to grow and learn. Now on the other hand, if there is abuse and dysfunction going on, it's important to find ways to get help for yourself. That's a circumstance in which you definitely would want to wish you were someone or someplace else. Throughout the years, I have had to make a variety of changes in my life. But whether it has meant pulling myself out of an abusive relationship or finding sobriety, my quality of life has improved as a result of those changes. So I highly recommend it.

We had a party tonight for a friend of ours who is off to Australia. She has fallen in love with an Aussie. We girls keep encouraging her to take it slow, but it's too late for that.

Coming from all of us who have rushed into things at least once, sometimes that's easier said than done. We just want the best for her.

March 22nd

I started a ten-day fast today. Marco is coming home from Fairhope and I told him I'm feeling the need for a fast, so he's going to do it with me. I tried it last year and I quite liked it. That may seem odd because you don't eat any solid food for ten days. We make a mixture of lemons, 100% maple syrup, cayenne pepper, and water. We make one gallon for each of us a day; sometimes I drink a whole gallon and sometimes less. It just depends. I work out and do all my regular tasks. You'd think you wouldn't have the energy, but you do. It's hard to explain. The only problem you encounter in the first few days is headaches, which are a result of detoxing from sugar and caffeine. But that will pass. I only drink two cups of coffee in the morning, but sugar is my weakness. The headaches haven't started yet, but they will. Fasting requires a certain type of discipline, and since I don't have to grocery shop, prepare meals, or do dishes, it leaves me with a lot more time in my day. I'm going to spend more time reading spiritual and uplifting material. Yes, the incense will be burning! The first time I fasted, I did it on my own. Believe it or not, I prepared meals for Marco and I didn't even have a taste! Maybe this time will be easier because Marco and I are fasting together. We'll see. Here we go.

I did the demo for "The Faithless Kind" today. Michael Smotherman, the song's writer, came to the studio and played keyboards on the demo. It was great to see him again. I first met Michael about ten years ago when he was living here in Nashville. Recently, he moved his family back to Detroit, his wife's hometown, so everyone can spend more time with her side of the family. He makes regular trips to Nashville, but it's been awhile since I've seen him. He mentioned Bonnie Raitt had recorded "The Faithless Kind" for an album that never was released. I'd love to hear her version. The demo went well, but I always need to digest everything and then listen to the song the next day to figure out how I really feel. But I'm glad that it's done. Generally, I liked the way my voice sounded on it. I'll see how I feel tomorrow.

March 23rd

I wrote with Patricia and Steve today. It went really well. We started a song called "I Wanna Go the Distance with You." I like it. We still have to write the second verse, but the general structure and music for the song is written. I went to a song-listening meeting this afternoon. I heard some really good songs, but no great songs. I did take a few songs, so that I can listen to them again when I get the compilation CD in the mail.

This is day two of the fast, and the headaches are beginning and my cough is still holding on. The nighttime is the toughest because we always have a snack in the evening while we're watching TV or a movie. Oh well, only eight more days to go.

Wow! I listened to the demo of "The Faithless Kind" and I think I did it in too low of a key. But I think my voice works well on it; we'll just have to find the right key. I am very fortunate that I have a good range in my voice from the bottom end to the top. But sometimes that can be a problem because it gives you too many choices. You just have to take the time to find the sweet spot. That means that you try a variety of keys. You'll know when you've found the right one.

March 24th

Day three. Get through day three and it'll set you free. I'm feeling good. I wrote with Colin Linden today. We almost finished our song. I like it. Colin brought a lot of the lyric and it's really interesting. The song is not one that you can take literally; it is more about the pictures the words represent, but the words do sing very nicely. I think it was Paul

McCartney who said that often a good song is just words that sing well. I asked Colin how he came up with the lyrics he brought for this song and he said that he gets inspiration in the morning and late at night and that he just tries to listen to his heart and not his head. I told him about writing this journal and that I'm trying to do the same thing. To just be open and follow my heart and not overthink things too much. That really is the balance I try to keep when being creative: to just come from my heart and not overthink.

We finished early because he had an afternoon appointment. I went to the gym and sat in the sauna and allowed my body to keep cleansing itself. It feels good.

March 25th

Got up early to do a 7 a.m. interview for a benefit show I'm doing on April 1 in Ottawa. The concert is a fundraiser for Lou Gehrig's Disease and I wanted to be sure that I had more information about the disease before I did the interview. Elizabeth Grandbois suffers from this disease and this is her benefit. It's called "Elizabeth's Concert of Hope." Elizabeth is a remarkable person: in the face of this disease she has raised 1.2 million dollars in four years. Lou Gehrig's Disease (known clinically as Amyotrophic Lateral Sclerosis or ALS) causes paralysis of the arms, legs, and the speaking and breathing muscles. Eventually, the person suffering is unable to communicate, unable to eat, and unable to breathe. About three thousand Canadians a year are affected by this disease, resulting in two to three deaths per day. The death rate for Lou Gehrig's Disease is comparable to AIDS. There is no treatment for ALS. I'm really glad we're doing this concert and that I can help raise awareness of this terrible disease.

There are so many needs out there, but I'm a firm believer that we all have to keep trying to do something to help when and where we can. I also really enjoy meeting courageous people like Elizabeth Grandbois. I'm inspired by her.

We went to the gym, and then, since Marco likes to go to

the movies in the afternoon, we took the opportunity to go and see *The Passion of the Christ*, Mel Gibson's movie about the Crucifixion of Christ. I wept through most of it. I'm going to need a day or two to process the movie. I know it's a great sacrifice for those of us who believe, but it was so difficult to watch. Even though I'm a Christian, I still have many questions and I still find some things hard to believe. But I'm choosing to have faith and to believe.

I organized band rehearsal for the Ottawa date. We're going to rehearse at Dan's house. He's my keyboard player. He's been with me for about fifteen years and he's like a brother to me. Dan has two little boys. He's such a great dad, but sometimes when it's time for rehearsals we have to work around his daddy duties, so going to his house is the easiest for him. That's fine with me. It's best for me if I do my songwriting and rehearsals away from my house because I get too easily distracted, what with the phone, or the animals, or whatever. We are going to perform in Ottawa as a four-piece and do an acoustic set. We haven't performed together since Christmas, so I'm really looking forward to seeing everyone and playing some music together. I really do have a gypsy soul. Although I've been getting that fulfilled somewhat traveling with Marco, I just enjoy getting on the tour bus or a plane and heading off somewhere with my band.

My brother, Steven, is visiting Mom in Arizona. I'm glad they're together. That will be good for them.

I can't wait to go and see my sister and her family. It's been since December and that's just too long. They were hoping to come for a visit earlier, but because they have started their own business it's too hard to get away right now. I sure understand. I'm getting such a kick out of talking to Bryanna on the phone because she is starting to put sentences together and it's fun having a real conversation with her. I called to tell her that I was coming for a visit and she got all excited because she thought it was today. I had to tell her to ask mommy to show her on the calendar when I was coming. It was so cute. Steven will be back from his visit with Mom, so I'll get to see him as well.

My mother Monica and my brother Steven.   Photographer: Julie Smith

March 26th

Day five of the fast. Marco has lost ten pounds; I've lost two. What's up with that? Sometimes it's hard to be a woman. But I'm glad I'm cleansing my body, although I still have a slight headache. I would imagine I'm on the last day of that. My cough is less intense, but it's still hanging on pretty good. Oh well. I'm glad I'm home and not having to do any public events.

I went and helped Marco set up for an Air Chair show here in Nashville. It's always great when he can work right here in our backyard, so he can come home at night. We then went and bought an iron gazebo with a cream-colored tarp cover and net curtains that can be closed to keep the mosquitoes out. We set it up and it looks great. While setting it up, however, we discovered that a few pieces were missing. I had to drive a one-hour round trip back to the store to get the parts, but we finally got the gazebo set up. I'm going to put wicker furniture in it and set it up all girlie like. It will be a nice place to sit and get away from the sun. We used to have a big shade tree in the backyard, but a tornado came through and took the tree with it. That was scary, and some of our neighbors lost a lot more than a tree, so we won't complain too much. (Although we did have six Air Chairs hanging under the tree and it was a great spot to hang out with our friends after a barbeque.) We're looking forward to getting the deck cover done, so we can hang a bunch of Air Chairs out there. I worked at hanging the curtains on the gazebo until the sun went down. It took a lot longer than I thought it would. Then I enjoyed a nice hot bath and afterwards we watched *The Sopranos*.

March 27th

I shopped all day for wicker furniture, cushions, indoor/outdoor carpet, and flowers. The gazebo looks fantastic! I am a real deal-shopper, so I tore this town up looking for exactly what I wanted and the best price.

March 28th

I went to the early service at church today. Marco had to go to work, but he has been spending time in meditation with God during our fast. He is feeling at peace; he feels that his walk with God is in a good place.

The service today was about patience. Generally, I tend to be a patient person. But sometimes I do find myself really challenged, especially when I want something now that I think would be good for me or my career, and it doesn't happen, no matter how hard I try to make it happen. But I have grown to learn that, without fail, everything has happened in my life when it should. That's why, for me, it's important to trust God and be patient. Things will happen as they should.

Pastor Foster made the analogy of a trapeze act, with one person the "catcher" and the other the "flyer". The flyer has to trust that the catcher is going to make the catch like he has so many times before. The two have a history not unlike we have with God.

My history with God has been that things, indeed, have happened as they should. "He has made everything beautiful in its time. He has also set eternity in the hearts of men; yet they cannot fathom what God has done from beginning to end." (Eccl 3:11-12 NIV.)

This passage reminds me of a particular event in my life and how I have come to trust God. A few years ago, while I was single, I was very interested in someone. I wanted to try to find a way to hang out with this person to get to know more about him. But no matter what I did, I couldn't seem to get hooked up with him or even be in the same room with him, for that matter. The next thing I knew, out of the blue I met Marco, and I couldn't imagine anyone more perfect for me. (Now that doesn't mean we have a perfect relationship, but pretty darn close.) Since then, the person I was originally trying to get hooked up with has been on his own journey of discovery (and not one with which I would have liked to have been involved). I wasn't looking for someone who was still discovering himself or still needing to sow his oats. I was looking for someone who had a pretty good idea of who he was and who was ready to settle down. And God brought me Marco.

I worked out in the yard until the sun went down. Came into the house and had a nice hot bath and drank some more lemon juice. Marco and I were laughing this morning because he made a new batch and after six days of drinking this stuff he said, "Mmm...this is a good batch!" It's a good thing we like lemon juice. It's been a full day and I'm tired.

March 29th

Patricia had to cancel our writing session today. She had a photo session come up that she had to do.

Marco and I went to the gym and then I came home and practiced my guitar to prepare for band rehearsal tomorrow. I am also finishing my journals.

Carolyn Dawn Johnson just e-mailed me while I was working on the computer. We haven't had a chance to talk or get
reconnected to work on the songs we started, and she is not
writing again until June or so because she is on the road doing
shows and promoting her new single. She's doing great, and
she's working hard.

March 30th

Band rehearsal went well with the guys today. We had a
chance to get caught up on everybody's lives and to organize
the next few days. We fly to Toronto tomorrow evening, and
to Ottawa early the next morning. All of that requires a bit of
organizing—getting everybody on the same page with respect
to departure and arrival times and all the rest.

After rehearsal I went to Famous Music for a listening session and I heard some really strong songs. I hope I still feel
the same way when I receive the publisher's cd compilation of
the songs I chose for further review.

Kyle has just finished the Restless Heart record. He's
taken off for a little vacation for a few days and then he'll be
going out to Santa Fe to listen to songs with Randy Travis. We
plan to get together on April 12 to listen to everything I have
written and all the songs we have found to determine where
we're at. I'm looking forward to that.

When I got home from my song-search appointment, a
new shipment of Air Chairs had arrived. Marco is getting
ready for two shows this weekend: he is setting up one of his
guys here in Nashville today, and then he has to load up for a
show in Texas. I helped him organize all of the new stock and
then reload for his Texas trip. He's leaving early tomorrow.

Marco's brother, Johnny, plays drums in a really cool band
called Calexico. They tour all around America, Canada, and
Europe. We went and saw them perform tonight at 12th &
Porter. It's a fantastic band. Not what you would call a com-
mercial band, mind you—their music is very original sounding

and sometimes the songs are five minutes long without the typical structure you hear in "commercially acceptable" music. They really resist all of that because they want to create music on their own terms (without anyone telling them how they should or shouldn't do it). My hat's off to them. They have a large following and they seem to be doing pretty well. You can check out their website at www.casadecalexico.com.

Today is day nine of the fast. Wow! We've almost made it! This time was harder then the first time for me. Maybe it was because I could smell all the neighborhood barbeques while I was outside working. We're feeling pretty tired, but we went out tonight. It's almost over.

March 31st

Got up early and helped Marco get everything ready for Texas. He left this morning.

This is day ten of the fast. It's a strange feeling because I'm glad it's almost over, but it also means that the challenge is over, too. I'm sure it will take me about two seconds to find a new challenge.

I've got everything ready that I need for my trip to Ottawa. The band, Brad, and I are meeting at the airport this afternoon. I'll write about all that after we land. I need to finish up a few more things around the house. I'm a bit concerned about flying on an empty stomach, but I'm feeling fine right now.

Well, we arrived safely in Toronto tonight, but it was quite the trip and I'm too tired to write about it right now. I'll fill you in tomorrow.

April 1st

Getting to Toronto last night proved to be more challenging than anticipated. The plan started to crumble early on when I got a phone call and it was Brad, my road manager, calling to tell me that the plane had been delayed. That wasn't such bad news—I could relax and get to the airport without worrying about running behind—because, as usual, I was running behind. (I seem to be perpetually late by fifteen minutes. Not for everything, just some things.) I arrived at the airport to learn that our flight had been cancelled, and that we would have to take a later one. We were booked on a direct flight to Toronto that would have arrived at 7 p.m., and we were planning to stay at a hotel right by Pearson Airport and fly to Ottawa in the morning. Instead, we took a flight with a connection in Cincinnati, getting in around midnight. I'm happy that at least we are going to be able to make it to the show.

So off we went, and as we approached Cincinnati and started to descend, my stomach started to churn and I broke out into a drenching sweat. I realized that my stomach hadn't had food in it for ten days. Lord help me if I started throwing up! I had the barf bag in one hand and I was fanning myself with the flight instruction brochure. I was thinking flying while fasting is NOT a good idea. I actually had thought about it before I flew, but I was feeling fine and didn't anticipate any problems.

Finally, we landed. I felt like I'd dodged a bullet and that I had better get something in my stomach before we took the connection to Toronto. I called Marco in Texas where he'd settled in, and I told him what had happened and that I needed to eat. Even though I didn't make it until the morning, we agreed that I'd succeeded in the fast.

I decided to have a turkey sandwich. I took a couple of bites and drank some orange juice. I started to feel better. We caught the connecting flight to Toronto. We got in around midnight and were up early this morning to head to Ottawa.

The flight to Ottawa was uneventful.

I called Marco when we landed and he told me he had a food confession to make. He said that while he was driving to Texas yesterday he stopped at McDonald's and later Burger King, and then he had pizza for dinner. Of course, I then had to make my food confession: that turkey sandwich I bought was not very good—particularly not as the first thing I got to eat in ten days—so I bought some salt and vinegar potato chips and ate those instead. Marco heard me out, and then calmly said, "April Fool." You could hear the delight in his voice. He didn't have any food confessions at all, but he got one out of me. What a brat!

The show tonight was just all right. We had been told that this was an acoustic event, but we ended up following a seven-piece rock band and we were closing the bill! I was concerned about the lack of energy that we would present with only our acoustic instruments, but there was nothing we could do about it.

We had our sound check in the afternoon and all went well. We use an in-ear monitor system, which means we no longer have amplifiers or floor monitors in our stage set-up. Everything we play or sing is heard through our ear monitors, which are shaped a lot like hearing aids.

So it was time for the show and we were standing back-stage, waiting for our introduction. But just as the emcee finished up with "here's Michelle Wright" and the stage curtain was about to rise, our ear monitors shut down. We couldn't hear anything. The audience was applauding and applauding. But we couldn't have the curtain raised because we couldn't hear anything so we couldn't perform.

We got a message to the announcers and they got out on stage to stall for time. In a couple of minutes, everything was working again. The introduction started anew...and again the ear monitors went down. The curtain was going up, and I was fit to be tied because I wanted to strangle whoever it was that couldn't figure out what was going on.

Finally, I could hear a single guitar in my ears. Nothing more, just one lonely guitar. I let the audience know that we were having some technical problems, but that I was there to sing for them. By this time, our crew had solved our monitor problems and all the instruments and voices miraculously re-emerged in our ear monitors. We did our show, but I hate to start that way; sometimes it's hard to regain your momentum and build the show the way you want to.

I know that I worry about these things more than I should, but we want to give our best to the audience every time. Our technical problems notwithstanding, audience feedback from the Ottawa show was really good, and I'm glad that everyone was pleased.

I learned a few lessons at this show. One of them is that from now on, when we're doing an acoustic set, I will always use floor monitors as well as ear monitors. Not only will I be able to hear the instruments if our in-ear monitors fail, but I think it might also help us on stage to avoid feeling so isolated by the ear monitors. We'll be able to feed off each other much better by using floor monitors.

I guess it's a question of balance. You see, about a year ago, after a benefit show I played in British Columbia, I made a decision never to go without ear monitors again. At that

Photographer: Julie Smith

show, because it was a benefit concert featuring many artists, most of whom—myself included—were not using their own bands, I chose to avoid dealing with the hassle of setting up my ear monitor system. Instead, I used the stage floor monitors that were there. Well, we didn't get a sound check and I ended up screaming over the band the whole show. I wasn't very happy with the way I sang. Then I found out that someone had recorded the whole show. I was very unhappy about that. I did not want anyone to have a copy of a show that I screamed through. So I decided I would never go without my ear monitors ever again. But now I know I'll never go without my "ears"—except when I'm doing an acoustic show. You just never stop learning.

I'm looking forward to my visit with my family tomorrow.

April 2nd

My flight to Toronto went well. Lori and Bryanna were there at the airport to meet me. Poor Bryanna was very sick. But she

My niece Bryanna.

showed her happiness to see me—and then she threw up.

It's so great to see my family. Since Lori had several errands to run, I tended to Bryanna. Then we went grocery shopping: we bought lots of fresh fruits and vegetables as well as salmon and chicken. I always whip up a big pot of vegetable soup and fresh salad, so it's there for the whole family to eat.

Brother Steven will be home from his visit with Mom tomorrow. I'm looking forward to seeing him and hearing about his visit with her.

I bought Bryanna a new CD and some new clothes. Kids' clothes are so cute, and Bryanna loves it when she gets new clothes. She is so adorable when she models them for us.

We had a quiet night, ate well, watched some TV, and settled in for a good night's sleep.

April 3rd

Steve came home from his visit with Mom today and it was so great to see him. He had a good visit with Mom. We all wish she would move back home, but, on the other hand, Tucson's a pretty nice place for her to be living in—especially when it's wintertime. It's just too hard to deal with the winters if she were to live in Ontario.

Every time I'm with my family I wish we lived closer so we could spend more time together.

Ed and Lori went out tonight to dinner and a party with some business associates. Steve and I watched the kids. Steve brought Cody a Mexican marionette from Arizona and we all got quite a kick out of getting it to work.

After we got the kids to bed, Steve and I played guitar together. That's something we haven't done for a long time. My brother taught me how to play guitar when we were kids. We had a kids' band with some of our schoolmates. Steve played guitar and I played drums. Then I decided I wanted to learn how to play guitar. Steve was taking guitar lessons and I wanted him to teach me some chords and things. I would shove cookies and crackers under his bedroom door to persuade him. Steve would usually teach me what I wanted to learn. But sometimes he'd just open the door and fire the cookies and crackers back at me. (In hindsight, I realize I was pretty persistent and wouldn't take no for an answer.)

Steve wanted to learn the new Keith Urban song "You'll Think of Me," so we worked on it and figured it out. It was fun except we were getting on each other's nerves a little bit, just like we did when we were kids, because he was hearing things one way and I was hearing things differently. When Lori came home she started laughing at us—we were acting just like her kids act with each other. Actually, we were having fun with each other more than anything else. It was just brother and sister antagonizing each other.

April 4th

We stayed up too late last night. When there are kids around, you get up when they want you to get up. I'm not used

My nephew Cody.

to that, but it was so cute to see Bryanna's face smiling at me when I woke up this morning. She was standing by my bed saying, "Get up, Aunt Michelle."

I took Cody to get his birthday present today. I won't be here for his birthday, but we've made it a tradition that if I'm around anywhere close to his birthday we go shopping together. It's so great being an aunt.

I miss Marco and wish he could be here, but he's having a good Air Chair show in Texas, so we're grateful for that.

We just hung out and did some housework today. It was a full day but a good day. All is well.

April 5th

I flew home today. The flight was uneventful. Marco came home from Texas. We ate pizza and watched *The Sopranos*. How fun is that!

April 6th

I wrote with Tony Hazeldon and Sarah Majors today. Tony is the songwriter who wrote "Take It Like a Man." It was great to see them both again. We've all been so busy with life that we haven't seen each other in a while. I've never hung out with Tony, but I've run into him here and there. I enjoyed writing with him today, and Sarah is always great to write with. We got started on something that seems to be interesting.

I'm not sure about Kyle and me doing this album together.

April 7th

I recorded demos all day today. We did a demo for "This Endless Night," which I wrote with Arnie Roman and Patricia Conroy, "I Believe," which I wrote with Carol Mack Parker and Patricia, and "In the Absence of Love," which I wrote with Lisa Brokop and Patricia. I'm not sure about any of these songs. My favorite is "This Endless Night." I'll have to wait until I hear the finished demos.

April 8th

I wrote with Sally Barris today. I'm a fan of hers. She's a great songwriter and a fantastic singer. The song is called "Out of the Blue." I like it. We'll see how it holds up.

I had band practice this afternoon. We're leaving tomorrow for a show in Edmonton. Everyone was in good spirits.

April 9th

We flew out to Edmonton today for the show. The flights were running a bit behind, but that's pretty much the way it goes. It's really amazing that we've never missed a gig due to flight delays.

The concert tomorrow night is for the country station CFCW. It's called a "listener appreciation party," a free show put on by a radio station for its audience. Listeners win their tickets by calling in to the station. It's a way for the station to have some fun with their loyal listeners and to say thanks. CFCW is celebrating its fortieth anniversary, and the station's management invited us to headline the festivities.

Adam Gregory is also on the bill, along with some other bands from the Edmonton area. I wonder how Adam is doing.

I'm looking forward to tomorrow night.

April 10th

The show went really well tonight. I like doing listener appreciation shows. It's fun for me as an artist. It gives me a chance to say thanks to the listeners, too.

I guess the only thing that was quite upsetting is that the dude supplying the show's sound gear showed up at the venue two hours late. Apparently, there was a misunderstanding about what time he needed to be there. I know how thorough Brad is in regards to his communication with the sound companies, so I'm afraid they dropped the ball.

I know it's important to recognize that we're all just human, but I get upset when things like that happen because I need everyone to be on time. Ours is a well-oiled machine that runs very smoothly, but when someone shows up two hours late, it puts everything behind. However, things all came together just

Photographer: Lise Monpetit

fine. My guys know how to get the job done.

The concert took place in the Shaw Conference Centre. During our sound check, I found out there was a cat show going on in the exhibit hall next to ours. I wandered over to have a look. I saw some really beautiful cats, including a variety of breeds I'd never seen before. I love animals. I've always had mixed-breed cats myself (Homer, Bart, Marge, and Caesar, to name a few of my kitties). My mother liked Siamese cats, though, and we had a few of that breed during my childhood.

I signed a lot of autographs after the show. Met some really fun people. Came back to the hotel and packed up for the morning flight.

April 11th

It's Easter Sunday. Another uneventful flight home. I spent some time on the flight remembering what this day represents for Christians and giving thanks. Marco had a bunch of Easter candy and eggs hidden around the house. Pat and Celeste came over. We had an Easter egg hunt, ate pizza, and watched the Lakers. They lost. We didn't find all the hidden chocolate, so I can look forward to a couple of surprises down the road when I'm cleaning. "Oh, the simple things in life."

What a fun day. I love chocolate, pizza, and basketball. It doesn't get any better than this.

April 12th

Cleaned the house and listened to songs.

April 13th

Mark Morton cancelled our songwriting appointment today. I'm actually glad that he did. When I have to work on weekends, I usually make Monday and Tuesday my weekend instead of Saturday and Sunday (which, of course, allows me time to do things that we all like to do on the weekend.)

My mom smokes. I'm so sad for her that she is having

such a hard time breaking the habit. I hate to say this, but I'm just waiting for the day when she tells us that she has cancer. She called me today to tell me that the doctor said she has a 95% chance of having a heart attack if she doesn't quit smoking. God, I hope she can quit. I know it's hard, but I also know, like any habit, you have to do it yourself. You have to be willing to do what you've got to do. You can't make the drinker stop drinking and you can't make the smoker stop smoking.

I got a lot of things done today. I have been told to accept the fact that everything will never all be done at the same time. The work of a woman is never done.

April 14th

I wrote with Sally Barris today. I like our song, but we have to keep working on it.

Gerald has a nice studio in his home, and we did a good demo of "In the Blink of an Eye" there tonight. We had a lot of fun together. I think this song will make the record.

I got home late. It's been a good day.

April 15th

I'm leaving tomorrow to do a couple of store openings in Ontario for TSC. Sean Smith, my lead guitarist, came over and we practiced for the shows. I do an acoustic presentation at the TSC store openings: Sean and I perform a bunch of my songs together, singing and playing our acoustic guitars on our own without the rest of the band. It's all that is necessary for these situations. It's really fun to do and it keeps my chops up when it comes to accompanying myself on guitar.

We had the builders come out and start the pergola on the deck.

I packed and I'm ready to go.

April 16th

Brian, Sean, and I flew to Detroit today. We were picked

up by limo and driven across the border to Windsor, where we'll stay the night. Tomorrow morning we drive to Essex, Ontario for the first TSC store opening and then fly by private plane to Listowel for the second event.

It's going to be an early morning, so I better get to sleep.

April 17th

I couldn't sleep last night. I don't really know why that happens, but I wish it hadn't happened last night. I had to get up at 6 a.m. to get ready for an 8 a.m. pick-up. John Couper, TSC's marketing director, met us at the hotel and off we went to the first show in Essex.

John's an easy guy to be around. He really takes care of business, so I can relax knowing that he and Brian have all the show details under control.

The first in-store went great. (Although, we did get there a little later than we had planned and my guitar wasn't working, so we had to take it apart and discovered that in the flight the electronics had been knocked loose. We got it fixed and the show started.) There were more than one thousand five hundred people there to celebrate the store opening with us, including my grandma, grandpa, and cousin Debbie.

We drove back to Windsor to catch the plane for Listowel. But first, of course, we had to stop for lunch at Harvey's. Harvey's is hands-down my favorite place to have a burger. I like their veggie burgers. It's a must stop whenever I come home to Canada. America doesn't have Harvey's. I think they need to open up a few down here.

Once I got on the plane I fell asleep and it felt so good. It was just enough to refresh me for the next in-store. It took us about one hour of flying to get there.

The second show in Listowel went great as well. Again, lots of people (about one thousand seven hundred fifty this time), and several hours of autograph signing.

We flew back to Windsor, drove back to Detroit, checked into our hotel near the airport, and here I am ready to sleep.

I don't think I'm going to have any problems sleeping tonight.

April 18th

I got up early and flew back home. The deck looks great. Marco already has Air Chairs hanging from the new pergola. We had a nice barbecue and spent a lot of time out there this evening in the Air Chairs relaxing and talking. I'm glad I married someone who's become my best friend.

Air Chairs and a new pergola.

April 19th

I had a music meeting with Kyle today. We are really struggling with songs. I'm getting concerned because the songs that I'm responding to, Kyle is not. We agreed that we need to go and take some listening sessions together. I look forward to spending time with him at some of these meetings to see what kind of songs we both respond to.

What makes this difficult is that as individuals we all respond to different songs, and I honestly think that women and men respond differently to songs. I know that for Kyle and me the most important thing is that I make the record I want to make, and if we are not responding to the same music, then that's OK. We'll both do the right thing.

April 20th

What a great day it is! Today is Marco and my second wedding anniversary and I couldn't be happier. Sharing my life with him is the easiest thing I do. I love him so much.

We agreed to not buy each other anything for our anniversary because we are doing some redecorating around the house—we just built the pergola on the deck, and we had to replace the air conditioner upstairs. We agreed that we would just go out to dinner. I should have known better. Marco bought me the most beautiful diamond earrings. He said he doesn't want his girl walking around without any "bling" on. Well, that made me laugh and cry. He also had a few of his favorite pictures of our wedding put into a really nice triptych frame. How cool is that! Not fair. I feel a bit silly because I didn't get him anything except a nice card, but I'm learning that when it comes to gifts and giving, Marco is a very generous and thoughtful man. Learning how to receive is another challenge for me sometimes, but one thing I'm sure of is that in the future there will be no more of these "let's not get each other anything" conversations.

We also are hoping to go to the beach, but until I get this next record finished, I'm not sure that I could take a week to ten days off somewhere and relax without thinking that I should be writing or looking for songs or something. But as soon as it is finished, we are beach-bound.

We went out for a fantastic dinner at Stoney River Legendary Steak House. The food was fantastic and I highly recommend it.

I also went to Famous Music with Kyle this morning and listened to songs. Glen Middleworth and his creative director, Curtis Green, played us some great material. It was a good day.

April 21st

I wrote with Tony and Sarah today. We almost finished our song. We had fun working together.

That being said, I'm really starting to wonder if I should change producers. I'm not sure that Kyle and I are on the same page as far as songs go.

April 22nd

I went to BMG with Kyle today for a listening session. I didn't hear anything special. I'm trying not to worry about it and to keep the faith that I will either write or find the songs. It's hard to explain what I'm looking for, but when you hear it, you just know "that's it." But until that happens, nothing happens.

I cooked and cleaned until midnight. Marco is working in town this week, so he gets to be home at night. I like it that way.

April 23rd

I went to Universal with Kyle today to listen to songs. Again, I really didn't hear anything.

I worked on the garden until 7 p.m. I put a new walkway in the garden and really tried to be very thorough with the weed-blocker cloth so that I can keep the weeds down. The Bermuda grass around here is nasty. (Crabgrass, for us Canadians.) If you don't keep it under control, it'll take right over. The garden looks beautiful, although it sure is hard work. I enjoy having my hands in the dirt. You can take the girl away from the farm, but you can't take the farm life away from the girl. I say that in fun, but I believe it. We worked really hard on the farm when I was growing up. I worked in the fields a lot, and I enjoyed it and still have a need for it. There is just nothing like a good day's work on the land. (Now I'm starting to sound like my grandfather.)

April 24th

I worked on the garden all day and got a lot done. I planted garlic for the first time and tomatoes, peppers, basil, dill,

Brussels sprouts, zucchini, and squash. Plus, I planted cantaloupe and watermelon for the neighborhood kids. I got almost the entire garden finished. I just have to put the plastic weed stopper down and the organic soil conditioner over that. It's great exercise, and I love having a garden of fresh vegetables to pick from. One of the simple pleasures of life for me.

I made a nice dinner for Marco and me. We really like salmon. Our good friend Mike Basow, who is a great cook, suggested that I cover the salmon in honey, wrap it in tin foil, and put it in the oven at 350 degrees for about twenty minutes. It's to die for. It's so good.

I'm journaling tonight, but I'm ready for some sleep.

April 25th

I worked on the garden and flowerbeds and spent time with God and nature. I didn't go to church, but I do feel connected.

Everything is looking beautiful around the yard. My diet is going well. I always get so much exercise when I'm working outside that it makes it easy to drop a few pounds and work a few muscles that haven't been worked out in a while. I also prepared a few days' worth of nice salads, fruit salads, and chicken, so we can eat on the run because this week is going to be very busy.

April 26th

I worked in the garden again today. I have about one more day to go.

I'm starting to really wonder if I should do the album with someone else and I'm sure Kyle is wondering the same thing. What makes this weird is that it's nothing personal. I have a great deal of respect for Kyle, and he has been nothing but professional. Actually, he has affirmed for me that there is a certain standard for doing business and that's just how it should be done; he has that kind of integrity. But we're just not connecting. We'll see, but I think this decision has to be made soon. Maybe he's just waiting for me to speak my mind.

I went shopping for Mike and Trisha's wedding gift today. Marco wanted to buy something that they did not register for, but I'm a firm believer in getting people what they register for rather than what you think they will like—unless it is a special piece of art or pottery or something like that.

We had a rehearsal with the PaJAMa Party tonight. It was great to see the girls and to sing together. I'm enjoying the friendships we are developing.

April 27th

I feel like I have finished up all the yardwork. Marco and I planted some new trees and all the deck furniture is out and most of the decorating is done. It looks great! I'm glad to have it almost finished. We obviously have longer summers down here than in the north, so we spend quite a bit of time outside and I like to make it look nice. Martha Stewart would be proud of me.

We had band rehearsal tonight and I came home and started packing. Since I'm going to be gone for five days, I have to take care of everything before I go. Marco is going to be home, so there is not as much to deal with. When we both go away, that's a different story.

April 28th

I finished packing and went shopping for wardrobe. I have such a hard time finding things that I want to wear on stage. It seems like a full-time job in itself! I used to work with a professional wardrobe consultant named Joan Lacey. Joan was originally hired by Arista Nashville, my record label at the time. We met on my first trip to New York in 1990. I went there to meet all the staff at Arista's Manhattan office and to get ready for the photo shoot for my first album. We did a lot of shopping. Joan was awesome. She's from New York and has a great sense of style. She's worked at a variety of fashion magazines in New York. I really trusted her taste.

I wasn't sure what to think about the Big Apple at first, though. It seemed all so fast-paced. I thought I was sure to die in a taxi accident the way those cab drivers screamed around town. I have since spent a lot more time in New York and I love it. I always look forward to my next trip there.

I haven't been touring as much in the last couple of years, so I decided it wasn't necessary to have a wardrobe consultant on salary anymore until things started getting busy again. But every time I go out shopping, I'm thinking it's time to hire someone again.

I do hire stylists on a per project basis, and it's fun to get them involved because they usually bring fresh ideas. Sometimes I'm resistant when I see a garment on a hanger. But then I try it on and I like it, although I may not have picked it out myself. It's actually a real privilege to have some-one shop for you. And it's often also necessary because there is only so much one person can do.

I flew to Calgary this afternoon and the flights were fine. It's nice to be in a quiet hotel room. Goodnight.

April 29th

I had a good night's sleep, got up, and went to the hotel gym. My diet and exercise program is going all right. I went shopping for wardrobe here, too, but I didn't find anything. I'm having a hard time finding something that I really like. I'm trying to find some unique stage clothes for the summer. A trip to Toronto or New York is in order.

The show tonight went really well and it was great to play with the band.

April 30th

The band flew back to Nashville today, but Brad and I flew out of Calgary to hook up with the PaJAMa Party. We all met at the Salt Lake City Airport where we jumped into a cou-ple of vans and drove to Idaho. Our show is tomorrow night.

I called Mike Basow today to wish him love and a peaceful day for his wedding. Tonight is the rehearsal and the rehearsal dinner. I wish I could be there.

I had a very interesting experience on the plane. I was writing in my journals and then I took my Bible out to read. The girl sitting beside me said she noticed I was writing journals and that I was reading the Bible. She asked me where I was coming from spiritually. She told me that she was really struggling. As a matter of a fact, she said, she was feeling suicidal. She really opened up to me, and I was able to share with her many of my own life's challenges and how I have found the most peace in reading the Bible and turning to God for comfort. I signed my Bible over to her, and I wrote some thoughts

Photographer: Lise Monpetit

in her journal, which I hope she will be able to refer to; hopefully, it may give her some source of inspiration.

I'm often amazed that we always seem to be where we need to be. She told me that she had tried to get on the plane the day before and that no matter what she did, she couldn't get on that plane. I guess we needed to be on the plane together. Maybe I couldn't be at Mike's wedding so that I could be on that plane and help someone through a difficult time. We both cried, and I gave her a way to contact me. I hope I hear from her.

The PaJAMa Party members all had dinner together tonight, and I'm ready for a good night's sleep. It's been a long day of travel.

May 1st

After a full day of rehearsal and sound check the show went well tonight.

Marco said that the wedding was really beautiful. I look forward to seeing the pictures.

May 2nd

I returned home late in the evening. All flights went well and it's good to be home.

May 3rd

I stayed home today and cleaned and organized. Did some laundry, some grocery shopping, and prepared a nice dinner and some salads. The regular routine. It always takes me a day or two when I get home off the road from a five-day trip to get everything taken care of and back in order.

May 4th

Had a listening session at SESAC this morning. I heard some good songs and one in particular called "Beautiful Today." I had already passed on this song because Kyle had previously recorded it with another artist and he wasn't particularly interested in revisiting it, but I find myself getting really emotional when I hear it. I have to pay attention to that.

I wrote with Margaret Findley today. I like the song and I enjoy writing with her.

May 5th

I wrote again with Margaret. We almost finished our song. It's called "It's Not Right."

May 6th

I listened to songs at home today and worked on a few ideas. I have to be honest: I'm really struggling with my songwriting. I don't think I'm being overly critical. I just don't think I'm writing very good songs. Every songwriter I talk to says you just have to keep on writing. I heard someone once say that writer's block is just an excuse for being lazy. That's pretty harsh, but I try to make sure I'm not just being lazy.

May 7th

I felt pretty low-energy today. I just laid low. Quite frankly, I'm feeling a bit depressed.

May 8th

Thank God it's the weekend and thank God for Marco. There is no one who can make me laugh like he does. Just his smile can lift my spirits. He has persuaded me to take it easy this weekend and not think or worry about much of anything. So that's what I'm doing.

May 9th

Today is Mother's Day. I love my mother so much. I'm truly amazed at the strength she showed as she raised us. Mom lost her own mother to a sudden illness when she was five years old, and life became very difficult for her after that. She was a single mother of two at the age of seventeen.

As I'm writing this, I don't want to go into too much detail. I would really need to talk to Mom. Maybe someday I'll write about it. I think it's really tough for children to be raised without their mother. Thank you, Mother, for all your love and strength.

Mom and I had a good conversation on the phone. She seems in pretty good spirits.

May 10*th*

All the girls from the PaJAMa Party individually are going to do a cooking show on the Great American Country TV channel called *Lorianne Crook's Celebrity Kitchen*. Lorianne used to co-host the *Crook and Chase* talk show that was on TNN. Anyone who is a country music fan will be quite familiar with that show.

I went to the grocery store and got all of the ingredients to prepare the recipe that I'm going to be making. I've chosen a salmon chowder that I found in the *South Beach Diet Cookbook*. I prepared it this evening and it's really delicious.

I'm looking forward to seeing Lorianne again. We've done a variety of interviews together over the years, but since the *Crook and Chase* show was cancelled, I haven't seen her around much. She was always a great interviewer and an easy person to be around.

Haven't been getting to the gym as much as I would like, but all my yardwork has been helping me burn up the calories and the pounds are coming off.

I'm continuing to gather songs and listen. I'm feeling encouraged by some of the songs that I've been finding, and I'm hoping that I can finish a few of the ideas that I'm working on.

I continue to be challenged by my own songwriting. It's a strange thing because I am very happy right now and in some ways, ironically, that makes it difficult to write. I've heard it said that unless you're struggling, it's difficult to write. Well, here I am, the happiest I've ever been and I'm struggling to write! Maybe there is some truth to that.

May 11th

The *Lorianne Crook's Celebrity Kitchen* appearance went really well today. We had a lot of fun, and it was nice to see Lorianne. The drummer from Confederate Railroad, Mark DuFresne, was also on the show, along with Andy Griggs.

Mark has his own cookbook out—I think that's great. A lot of guys love to cook. Guys that I would not in the least expect to be having conversations with about a favorite recipe. Girls, I think we need to encourage our men to cook more. (Just imagine if you didn't have to prepare most of the meals. Maybe then we could have a few more hot baths.)

We went to Kevin Ferriman's school awards show tonight at Father Ryan High School in Nashville. Much to our delight, Kevin was awarded a full year's scholarship for his excellence in music and for his leadership in the school's marching band and winter drum-line program. It really makes me proud for Kevin and his family. It's great to see Brian and Sue shine with pride—not because of the award, although I'm sure a full-year scholarship would make any parent smile—but because this was something that Kevin worked so hard at for himself. He has shown a high level of discipline plus a keen desire to learn and achieve at the highest level, and he's done that. That's admirable.

I'm glad that Marco could be at the awards as well. I've known Kevin since he was born, and it's good when Marco can spend some time with the Ferriman family as well and develop his relationship with them, too.

May 14th

Big news! I've made a decision to do my next album with Tony Hazeldon and Russ Zavitson. Brian and I had a meeting this morning with the guys to discuss some of the details. TSC has asked me to make a Christmas album exclusively for their stores, and I would like Tony and Russ to produce that CD as well, so we have a lot to talk about and a lot of work to do. Based on our meeting, I would like to move forward with these guys.

I'll have to speak with Kyle about this, but I think he's feeling the same way. We have always been very professional and straightforward with each other, so I feel confident that our relationship is on solid ground. It's nothing personal—just different creative points of view.

I wrote with Sally Barris again today. She just got back from touring in England for the past month. It was good to hear her talk about her experience there. I've performed in the United Kingdom. It's so great to have those kinds of experiences in different countries.

No matter what country I'm in at the time, I keep concluding that we all have the same basic needs—hopes and dreams for love and a good family—whether it be in Africa or Germany. I'm not going to talk a lot about what's going on in Iraq because I don't feel particularly well informed, but I sure hope the families who are living over there will someday enjoy freedom and the ability to dream.

After a quick stop at Back Yard Burgers for a veggie burger for dinner, I had an evening writing session with Cyril Rawson and Darryl Burgess. They're a couple of fine young Canadians. We started a really cool song. It's called "Rose Colored Sky."

I got home late. It's been a long day, but a good one. I'm having a yard sale tomorrow. To some people reading this, me having a yard sale may just sound crazy, but in my neighborhood I'm just one of the neighbors, and yard sales are very common in the south. I just throw on a baseball cap and my sunglasses, and, with few exceptions, no one recognizes me.

I live in a very nice neighborhood, but I don't live in a mansion and I am also very frugal. It would be silly for Marco and me to be living in a house any bigger than the one we have.

Today I have decided to get rid of all the plastic plants in my house. I cannot believe how many plastic trees and plants I have. One of the trees is sixteen feet high! I guess I'm just over the plastic phase in my life. Marco was cute when I told him that. He just gave me a hug and said, "I am so happy to hear that because I never really liked the plastic plants." It's taking a little getting used to, because there is no longer a plastic tree in every corner, but the house does look very clean and uncluttered.

I also went through all of my drawers and closets today as well as my beautiful award-show gowns that are a size two. Can you believe that? A size two. I can't get them over my knees. I'll use some for charity and some I'll keep for memories. Or maybe I'll lose enough weight and...Oh, never mind. I've married an Italian and life's too full to worry about being a size two forever.

Speaking of Italian, Marco knows how hard I've been working these last few days to get everything cleaned up and organized, so he made Convertino pasta sauce, and even though I've had my share tonight, my mouth is watering as I type this. It's just that good.

Living the good life. Marco making his famous Convertino pasta sauce.

I found out today that I have an opportunity to go on another trip with World Vision, this time to Honduras. I really want to go, but part of me is wondering if I'm prepared to cope with the emotional toll of the experience.

The trip to Honduras would be in early June. Around that time Marco and I are planning a full Convertino family visit (which means thirteen people from his side as well as my cousin Debbie), and it's Fan Fair in early June. I will have only been home for two days from the mission. I'm concerned I'll still be recovering from it all.

I know I'm going to do the mission, but I'm a bit surprised by my hesitation. Or maybe it's just the recognition that if I do this, it will take its toll. But certainly the payback is in knowing that my participation will ultimately help make a difference for the children.

I really wanted to be able to bring Marco with me on my next World Vision mission, but he has to work. Sometimes it's hard to explain what happens to you when you go on a trip like this, and I would like to share this life-changing experience first-hand with Marco some day.

May 15th

The garage sale went great. I got rid of just about everything. And I got the garage cleaned out, too!

My cat Marge is missing and I'm very concerned. I'm in bed right now as I'm typing this and she usually crawls right in with me.

I've had three other cats disappear and I just hate the thought of something happening to her. Marge is thirteen years old and very fragile. I'm thinking she may have climbed into the car of someone who stopped for the yard sale. This is a habit of hers. As a result, and especially in the heat of the summer, we always check our cars when we close the doors after unloading groceries or whatever to make sure Marge is not trapped inside.

One time, Marco was driving to Texas and, sure enough,

out pops Marge, so he had to drive back home. Fortunately, he was only a few miles down the road.

I did some more work outside. Apart from Marge's disappearance, it's been a long but good day.

May 16th

Thank God for Sundays at home. We got up and went to the early church service and came home and I made pancakes. We also watched basketball and ate Italian cream cake. (This was definitely the binge day. I'm finding that having one day a week to eat what ever I want is working for me! I remember Terri Clark telling me that that's what her trainer suggested she do, and I think it's not a bad idea.)

Marco suggested we take Gracie for a walk to burn off some of our food indulgences before we started watching *The Sopranos* and going for round two (finishing up the Convertino pasta and, of course, the Italian cream cake). It was a beautiful night. As we were walking, we started seeing signs posted that said "gray cat found." Well, my heart sank because Marge is not gray, but we took note of the phone number on the signs and continued our walk. I wanted to go home right away and call, but since the description didn't seem like it was Marge, we kept on walking. As soon as we got home, we called the number and I started to describe Marge. I asked if the cat had white paws and the man who had answered said "yes." Then I asked if the stray was a female and the guy said "yes." So I told him her name, and he called her and she looked at him. Well, I couldn't believe it. Could it be our kitty? We jumped in the car and drove to his house and, sure enough, it was Marge.

I feel the tears coming to my eyes as I'm writing this because I am so happy that she's all right. The two little children who lived in the house were the ones who found Marge; they were the ones who put up the signs around the neighborhood, went and bought her cat food, and took care of her. They actually looked a little disappointed when we arrived to pick her up. I think they wanted to keep her because she's such a sweet cat. I dropped off a thank-you note and a little reward. I'm so glad they took care of her. Now we have five bodies back in our bed.

May 17th

Got up early and went to the gym. I wrote with Mark Morton at his house. We started a cool song.

I'm going to Moncton, New Brunswick, on May 25 to film a television show. I always enjoy going to Atlantic Canada and hanging out with the Maritimers.

Sean, my guitar player, has a side business painting houses. I have hired him to come over and paint our place. I will help him, so we can get it done in one day.

May 18th

I had another meeting with Tony and Russ this morning. We are going to the studio to try a few things just to see how we work with one another. I don't anticipate any problems, but you never know. It's better to be safe than sorry.

I called Kyle, and we agreed that making an album together would not be the right thing to do. We're both disappointed, but I feel like the conversation ended positively.

Sean is painting the house and I will help him tomorrow.

May 19th

I painted the house with Sean today. It took us the entire day, but we got everything finished. I've been living here almost ten years and it's the first time the house has been painted. I could see a few spots where the paint had worn off, and if we didn't get it painted, the wood would have rotted.

May 20th

Today, I went shopping for a variety of things for the house. I was going to go out for only a couple of hours, but I decided to see how much I could get done, and I got home pretty late. That shopping will wear you out.

May 21ˢᵗ

I'm going to work on the house for the next few days. We are going to do some interior painting and redecorating.

May 22ⁿᵈ

Working on the house.

May 23ʳᵈ

Working on the house.

May 24ᵗʰ

I went in the studio today with Russ and Tony to see how we felt working together. It was great. Tony and Russ are so easy to be around.

We recorded a wonderful song, "Will You Love Me Anyway?" It tells the story of a woman who is dealing with having waited too long before trying to have children. Now she may not be able to. I know a lot of women in similar situations.

I think it's a great song. A good friend of mine, Sarah Majors, wrote it. I first met Sarah when I hired her to play and sing in my band during a Canadian tour we did in 1995. She fell in love with my drummer at the time, Pasi Leppikangas, and they got married a couple of years later. She's been a real inspiration for me as a songwriter.

May 25ᵗʰ

I left for Moncton today to tape a television show called *Pour L'Amour du Country*, which will air on the Canadian Broadcasting Corporation's French network later this year. It was a full day of flying and I'm glad to be here in my hotel room safe and sound. I can't get cell-phone service here, so I won't be able to talk to Marco as often as I'd like. Marco and I always talk several times a day. We often wonder what people did before cell phones. Now I know—they missed each other.

May 26ᵗʰ

The show taping went well. Afternoon rehearsal, with an evening taping before a live audience. I did two shows. In the first show I sang "Take It Like a Man" and "I Surrender." For the second show, I sang "Guitar Talk" and "Every Time You Come Around." It was nice working with the other guest artists and I enjoyed the relaxed atmosphere on the set.

There has been some talk about me having my own music television show, similar to *The Tommy Hunter Show*. The concept of having a music show is really intriguing. The only hesitation I might have is that anything I do outside of singing, writing, and recording has to be right; the only way to know is to do it and put it out there and hope that the public likes it. You have to be prepared to fail in front of the public.

May 27ᵗʰ

Another full day of flying. It was uneventful. I'm looking forward to getting home and finishing the house. The good thing about having company is that it forces me to do a few things that I would otherwise continue to put off.

May 28ᵗʰ

I did a lot of housework today.

May 29ᵗʰ

Marco and I went on a pontoon boat with a group of friends and had a great time. Since the family is arriving in a couple of weeks, Marco and I are trying to get all our work done around the house.

May 30ᵗʰ

Church and housework.

May 31ˢᵗ

Today is a holiday, so it's quiet around here. I painted a

wall in the living room. The color is burnt red, so it's going to take three coats. I forgot about that. And you should always use a primer tinted the same color as the paint you are applying. I didn't do that.

I'm also getting ready for my trip to Honduras. I've brought out the clothes I wore in Africa. They are made of material that is more heat- and water-resistant than what I would ordinarily wear. In fact, I don't wear these clothes for any other reason. Their style is not exactly in vogue!

June 1st

I had another music meeting with Tony and Russ today and further discussions about budgets for both albums. We have to decide where we are going to record the projects, and what songs and musicians will be a part of it all.

I finished packing for Honduras. I have to pick Brian up at 5 a.m., so it will be an early night.

June 2nd

Brian and I made it to the airport on time and all our flights went well. We hooked up with some of the World Vision team in Miami, and then we flew into Tegucigalpa, Honduras. Apparently, this is a particularly tricky landing— the airport is nestled amongst the mountains—but our pilots did a great job. I've been involved in worse landings.

I am doing this trip with a couple of media personalities from Winnipeg. Sylvia Kuzyk is the CKY-TV News weather anchor and Ron Able is the on-air morning host at QX 104.1 FM radio. I've done a few interviews with both of them, so it will be nice to get to know them better and to share this life experience with them.

As we were landing, you could clearly see hundreds of run-down shacks built into the hillsides. I have seen housing like this before in some of my other travels (in the Dominican Republic and Venezuela, for example), so I wasn't as shocked and unprepared as when I first saw such evidence of poverty.

The first time I encountered such wretched living conditions I couldn't believe people lived like that. They were so poor, with so little help—and this was all there was. It's so heartbreaking. Seeing those shacks as we were landing started to prepare me for what lay ahead in Honduras.

We were greeted at the airport by some of the staff working for World Vision in Tegucigalpa. We all piled into a van and drove to the hotel.

At first glance, Tegucigalpa seems like a pretty normal city: lots of traffic, fast-food restaurants, billboards, and bustle. We're staying in a nice hotel across from a big mall where we shopped for a variety of things for the families that we meet tomorrow. Then we went out for dinner—to a Tony Roma's of all places!—but I know that tomorrow we will be entering a very different world.

When traveling abroad, always be very careful of what you eat and drink. I avoid eating any uncooked vegetables (that puts salads and tomato sandwiches out of consideration for me), and I never eat any type of meat or fish when I'm in a country outside of North America. I was hoping to find some pasta, but I ate cooked vegetables and French fries tonight. A good excuse to eat some fries, I suppose.

I've been looking forward to the trip, but I am concerned about its effects on me. It's not easy to see people suffering. But I do find some peace in knowing that I'm doing my part and I'm grateful that charitable organizations call on me to help.

I've got my clothes ready for tomorrow morning and I'm going to watch some TV and go to sleep. I don't know what to expect tomorrow, but I do know we're going to help a few families.

June 4th

We all met at 7:30 this morning for breakfast and then loaded into a van to head out to the first site. We parked at a gas station and walked to a shantytown built into both sides of a quarry-like valley with a polluted stream at the very bottom.

The smell and the deplorable conditions are unimaginable. There are about two thousand families living in the community.

The first family that we visited was Julio's. He and his wife, Jennifer, have three young children: Jose Mario, an eight-year-old boy; Genesis, a two-and-a-half-year-old girl; and Lucero, a four-month-old baby who doesn't stop smiling and giggling. The baby was so cute and of course has no idea about the sad circumstances into which he has been born.

We sat down with an interpreter and talked to Julio and Jennifer. The couple once enjoyed a much different life. Julio, who is forty-five, brought out his photo album and showed me pictures of how it used to be for the family. He was a personal bodyguard for a member of the government and he did a lot of traveling in North America and Europe. But one of the big problems in Honduras is the gangs: they burned his house down, and he had nowhere to flee except to this area. Ever since, Julio has struggled to get back on his feet.

The valley where they live is a patch of free land anyone can build on. Many of the city's poor have brought their last few remaining possessions here and built shacks out of whatever materials they can find (or afford to buy based on the small amount of money that some of them are able to earn. Julio makes wooden toys and occasionally manages to sell a few on the city streets up above the valley).

Julio and Jennifer's tiny one-room home has a mud floor, thin plywood walls, and a tin roof riddled with nail holes. Julio has tried to cover as many of the holes as he can, but the rain still gets through and it's difficult to keep the few things they own in reasonable condition.

The stream running through this valley is an open sewer for the community. Children and animals often become very sick due to the unsanitary conditions. Adults know to avoid the stream, but it's difficult to keep the children and dogs away. The kids just want to play, but it's impossible to keep track of your kids all the time. Many of the valley children have asthmatic symptoms—coughing and wheezing. And there's no money for medicine.

As I'm writing this, I'm realizing that this is the only choice these people have. But that being said, they are also trying to keep their dignity at the same time. These are real people, not so different from you or me, just down on their luck and desperately in need of help.

We asked Jennifer what hopes she had for the future of her children. She started to cry; she could hardly speak. Seeing that kind of heartbreak changes you forever. She hopes that some day they can move out of this valley. (By now Brian and I are calling it "The Pit of Hell.") Someone mentioned that sixty of the families are to be relocated to a much better section of the city, an area with newly built cinder-block homes, proper sewage, and running water. I hope Julio's family is chosen for relocation, but there is no way to know at this time. But at least the relocation program is a start, and for the families that are picked, it represents a whole new beginning that may bring hope back into their lives.

Jennifer and I had a chance to talk off camera with the help of an interpreter. We talk quietly, woman to woman. Jennifer has a kind heart, but at thirty years of age, she's a broken woman. I'm full of great sadness for her.

The story we are filming today is based on their daughter, Genesis. She seemed a bit overwhelmed by everything, so after we were finished talking with Julio and Jennifer, I spent time holding Genesis and playing with her as the cameras rolled. She really warmed up to me and I had a chance to enjoy her hugs and laughter. So innocent.

I decided that I would like to sponsor Genesis. We returned to the hotel for a couple of hours before our afternoon visit with another family in the valley. I called Marco and of course he agreed with my idea. We also decided to donate a mere $150 to Julio, so he can put a new waterproof roof on the shack his family calls home.

When we returned to the valley and I gave Julio the money for his roof, he put his head in his hands and sobbed.

A Honduran shantytown.   Photographer: Phillip Maher

A very powerful image I won't ever forget. The World Vision people said they'd send me a picture of the home when the roof repair is finished.

We then met a second family living in the valley. Victoria is a nineteen-year-old girl living in a shack right by the stream with her two sons, Anthony, five, and Michael, three, and her eighty-two-year-old blind grandmother. The grandmother got a virus in her eyes sixty years ago and lost her sight. She has lived in this community for most of her adult life. Like Julio, Victoria lived in a much different environment not too long ago. But her boyfriend (the father of her children) started to abuse her and she had nowhere to go except here.

In speaking with the World Vision people it appears that Victoria, like so many Honduran single mothers, is caught up in a vicious circle. To support her family, she needs to work. But in order to be allowed to work, she needs to get her health and working certificates, which cost about $125 to obtain—an amount that Victoria simply does not have. Victoria has no education or work experience, and the only way to get either one is with financial help. Moreover, her certification has to

Genesis. Photographer: Phillip Maher

be updated every year. It's an impossible situation. At nineteen, Victoria could already be at the end of her road—this is what the rest of her life could look like.

Victoria and her family share their shack with her cousin Linda, her husband, and their two kids, one of whom, five-year-old Jose, thankfully has begun to receive World Vision sponsorship. But the shack is very crowded. When it rains, the stream floods the shack, and whether it's the middle of the day or the middle of the night, all seven family members have to scramble to higher ground, to a tiny temporary shelter built into the hill by Linda's husband. Conditions are very tough.

Brian and I are having an ongoing conversation about what we're observing here in Honduras. We're both angered and saddened by the contrast between the haves and the have-nots. When we visited rural Zambia, the evidence of poverty, disease, drought, and despair was widespread; it seemed like the whole country was downtrodden. But the residents of this Honduran Pit of Hell live only a few hundred yards away from some significantly affluent areas: poverty and great wealth visibly co-exist here—an ironic fulfillment of the New World's promise? It's a world informed, we suspect, not by compassion, but by indifference. I don't understand how this can be, but that's one reason I'm here: to observe, learn, and, hopefully, understand. Perhaps then I can help other people understand as well. But I feel a long way from understanding right now.

June 5th

Today was a good day from the standpoint of having an opportunity to see World Vision at work. We traveled to another part of Tegucigalpa and visited the home of Norma Ortiz, a mother of two with a daughter, Mayra, who is sixteen, and a son, Nestor, who is eight. Norma cleaned houses for a living, but she contracted AIDS and became too sick to work and almost lost her job. But she showed a courage and strength that is admirable. She fought the system with the

Mayra: healthier and happier with the help of World Vision Canada.
Photographer: Phillip Maher

help of World Vision: her employers were persuaded to hold her job for her until she could be given the medicine needed to ease her symptoms. World Vision stepped in, obtained the medicine she needed, and after some months, Norma was able to go back to work.

In addition, World Vision built the family a two-room cinder-block home with a cement floor, locks on the doors and windows, a kitchen area with a refrigerator, running water, an exterior shower, and a modern sewage system. The house was very clean; you could tell that Norma took pride in her home. I was so glad to see this, and to know that this family has a real floor to walk on; clean, dry bedding to sleep in; and doors that can be locked at night.

Her daughter has been able to go back to school as well. When Norma first fell ill, Mayra was so concerned she couldn't concentrate at school. Rather than leaving her mom alone in bed to suffer, she would skip school to take care of her. Although Norma still has her bad days, all in all, thanks to World Vision, things are much better for this family.

Nestor, the young boy in the home, has been a sponsored child for a few years. There is such a difference in how he looks compared to some of the other children from yesterday's site visit. Nestor's health is good. He has school clothes and books, and he's quick to laugh and play. When Norma was interviewed, she couldn't express her thanks enough to World Vision and the people who have helped her to survive and be there for her children.

We then visited some hospitals and health care centers to see first-hand the care World Vision is providing for the community. At one World Vision facility, we were introduced to several families with sponsored children. Once again, compared to yesterday, there were more smiles and healthier children. The kids showed us some letters and pictures they'd received from their sponsor families.

There was a soccer field right next to the building, and, after watching the kids for a while, I joined in and got to play some soccer, too! It was really enjoyable. The World Vision crew set up their cameras and tape recorders nearby and did some concluding interviews with Sylvia, Ron, and me. They wanted to know how we were feeling. I had a hard time expressing myself. It's difficult to process everything in such a short amount of time, but I'm glad to be here and I'm glad I've had a chance to see for myself the help and hope that World Vision's programs can offer.

We returned to the hotel and met for dinner. Later in the evening a number of us got together to wind down from the emotional intensity of the past two days' activities. Some interesting and somewhat heated conversations ensued. Conversations about terrorism and religion, for example— conversations that I enjoy having because they allow me to hear a variety of viewpoints. It's amazing to me how passionate we all are about our opinions, and how disparate they can be. I often hesitate to say much because I know that none of us has all the facts, but I do remain interested in people's opinions and points of view.

On a family note, Cousin Debbie is arriving today in Nashville. She will be picking up Gracie from the kennel and watching over the house until I get home. Marco arrives home from Texas on Monday afternoon.

We leave Honduras tomorrow. I'm still processing all I have seen over the last couple of days. I am glad to be here. And I know, without a doubt, that this is the right thing to do—encouraging people to sponsor these children, knowing that, at the very least, through World Vision, we can ease some of their suffering.

June 6th

We're flying home today and I'm processing everything I have just experienced. I'm so saddened by all the suffering, and I'm really confused by it. How can people in countries like Honduras—particularly the governments and the wealthy—be so passive? I'm now more aware than ever before of the greed and lack of concern for our fellow man that's out there in the world. That being said, I'm really happy to be associated with an organization that is striving to make a difference.

Fan Fair week, or its new name, the Country Music Association's Music Festival, starts tomorrow in Nashville. The first thing on tomorrow's agenda is a television interview with the rest of the PaJAMa Party on the Channel 4 *News at Noon* show. We're going to do the show in our pajamas. I don't have any pajamas that I would wear on TV, so I'll have to go shopping tomorrow morning.

I'm looking forward to the family visit. And my godson, Joey, is arriving for his annual summer visit as well. I hope I'm able to handle and enjoy everything that's sure to be going on. Our flights were delayed: we got home at midnight instead of 6 p.m. I'm pretty tired, and we have to get up early to go shopping. I'm glad to be home safe. Marco had a good show in Texas, and Debbie is all settled in. I'll deal with tomorrow when it gets here. Goodnight.

June 7th

Got up early, organized a few things, and headed out to

shop for pajamas. What a nightmare that was. I wanted a certain style. Of course, it was really hard to find. But eventually I found something that I was comfortable in, especially for TV. I've never been on TV in my pajamas before. It was great to see the girls and we had a lot of fun on the show. We've got a lot of work to do together this week, and I'm looking forward to it.

Six of Marco's family members will be arriving in a couple of days. I've got to get their rooms ready upstairs, but we'll start that tomorrow.

Debbie and I spent some time together and prepared a nice meal for Marco when he got home. I really missed him while I was away. I'm glad we're all home safe. Now I need to get a good night's sleep.

June 8th

Well, I got a lot done today. I had several beds to make up and several rooms to dust and vacuum. I've got all the sheets and feather beds and air mattresses ready and I'm going to make up all the beds tomorrow morning. The family's due to arrive in the afternoon.

Debbie and I are going to spend some more time together tonight. After that, my schedule is going to be pretty divided for the next few days: from the family visit to Fan Fair, spending quality time with my godson to doing some PaJAMa Party shows in Indiana and Ohio at the end of the week. I'll be running. Tonight I'd better enjoy the quiet before the storm.

June 9th

Oh, my, what a day this was! We got up early so I could run some last-minute errands before focusing on making beds and getting the house ready for the family visit. I had made a decision last night not to worry about having everything perfect. Besides, I've got all day because the family is arriving in the afternoon, right? Wrong.

While Debbie and I were at the grocery store, Marco called and said, "Surprise! Six of the family are at the airport." Now, keep in mind, it's 9 a.m.

Marco's brother-in-law George works for American Airlines, so the gang coming in from Oklahoma (George and his wife, Charisse, Marco's sister; their three kids, Jordan, Caitlin, and Eliot; and Marco's mom, Glenna Jeanne) flew standby. They had no idea they'd be able to catch the first flight out of Oklahoma at 7 a.m. and then the first connecting flight out of Dallas. Normally, flying standby they would have had to wait on at least one of these flights, but there they were in Nashville at 9 a.m.

I couldn't believe it. Marco explained helpfully, "I've got the vacuum out and I'm almost done washing the floors and I've asked them to grab a sandwich and a cold drink and we'll be there as soon as we can."

Debbie and I raced home and threw all the sheets on the beds, and then Marco and I took off to the airport in separate cars while Debbie finished up the last few things at the house. My car is in the shop for regular maintenance, and, as always, my dealership has given me a loaner. While I'm en route to the airport, they call to tell me my car is ready. The dealership is on the way, so I decided to pick up my own car, meet the gang at the airport, go straight home, and start the party. ("Commence-O Festival," as we say at our house.)

I got my car. It's running fine, and we get the first group of family members picked up. It's so great to see them all.

As we were driving home, we noticed the air conditioner in my car doesn't seem to be working very well. It's a typical June day in Nashville—hot (about ninety degrees) and *really* humid—but I wanted to get everyone home and then deal with the car. In the meantime, I had an advance phone-in radio interview to promote a PaJAMa Party show we're playing next week in Minnesota and I had to do it while we were driving home. Now, normally this would be just fine, but as I'm doing the interview, the car kept getting hotter and hotter, and we couldn't roll down the windows because I wouldn't have been able to hear the interviewer. I'm thinking, "OK, this will be short and sweet and then we can roll the windows down." Well, the interviewer happens to be a real supporter of my music, and it'd been a while since we'd talked, so here we are, live on-air, and it's really a great interview, but everyone's dying in the car, and I didn't want to be rude to the interviewer, and I didn't know what to do. Finally, we pulled into our driveway, and we all rolled out of the car, and I finished the interview standing in my backyard while Marco brought everyone into the house to cool them down.

All right, so that's done. Not exactly the way I was hoping to start our visit, especially since this is the first time Marco's family has been to our home, but c'est la vie. Then someone reports that it's eighty-eight degrees upstairs where our guests are all going to be sleeping. We had just put in a new air conditioner upstairs about two months ago, but it decides not to work today. I call the air conditioning people and they assure me they will be there in a couple of hours to fix it.

Now I need to deal with the air conditioner in my car. I call the dealership and they suggest I bring the car back in. Marco gets everyone settled, and Debbie and I head back to the dealership. But about halfway there the car stalls, and Debbie asks, "Is that dial supposed to be on the 'H'?" I have no idea, but the car starts up again and we almost make it to the dealership. It literally stalls out as I'm turning into the lot. We coast to the service door, and the car is totally dead. They give me another loaner and I can't help but think about the cost of replacing my air conditioner. I drive a Mercedes: it's been a good car for me, but repairs certainly aren't cheap.

We get home, and the air conditioner people have fixed everything upstairs and it's starting to cool down. Good! Now the seven people who are going to be sleeping upstairs will be comfortable.

The girls decide they want to unpack, so they head upstairs. But the outlets are not working in the bathroom.

We have no idea why, so we run an extension cord from another room and everything is fine...until the phone in the kitchen breaks, and every time the phone rings I have to run to our bedroom to answer the phone that's working in there.

I decide to bring the bedroom phone into the kitchen because none of the phones upstairs have caller ID and I never answer the phone unless I know who's calling. Of course, just as I'm back in the bedroom, the phone rings. But the phone is now in the kitchen, so there I am running back and forth, and this just happens to be one of the busiest times of the year here in Nashville because it's Fan Fair. We have to go buy a new phone, but I'll do that tomorrow: right now I have to get ready to go to a rehearsal for the PaJAMa Party show we're doing at Fan Fair. Then, just as I'm getting ready to leave for the rehearsal, the toilet upstairs breaks!

At this point, Marco and I are close to hysterical because normally life around here is smooth sailing—but not today. There are a few other bathrooms in this home, so we'll be fine until tomorrow.

By now, Marco's brother Johnny has arrived from Arizona with his daughter, Mia; Camille is in from New Mexico; and Marco's sister Celeste and hubby, Pat, who live here in Nashville, have shown up as well. That's a total of fourteen people in the house. We're all having a laugh about the crazy day, but it's so great to have everyone here. The Convertinos are my kind of people, and I'm impressed at how calm Marco and I have stayed through it all.

Rehearsal with the PaJAMa Party was fun. It was great to see Deborah and Heather and Jennifer and the band guys. We have a lot of fun together and it was a nice way to end a pretty crazy day. All I can hope is that that's it. Goodnight.

June 10th

I slept in this morning and had a nice breakfast with everyone. Then I went to pick up my godson, Joey, at his dad's house in Nashville. It is always great to see him. He's getting so big. He's just turned thirteen and he's almost taller than me now. He's going to be spending a couple of days at our house with the rest of the gang.

This afternoon, I went to a Fan Fair event in downtown Nashville. The marketing people from Crisco, working with the Country Music Association (CMA), have put together a promotional cookbook for Fan Fair 2005 featuring the favorite recipes of a number of country artists, including Vince Gill, Brad Paisley, and Loretta Lynn, among others. I was invited to participate, so I submitted my recipe for a delicious breakfast pastry called palacsinta. My mother taught me to bake it when I was growing up. Marco loves it, but I only make it on Christmas morning. Since he asked me to marry him on a Christmas Day, I'm convinced the palacsinta had something to do with it. Just kidding...sort of. Over fifty thousand of these cookbooks will be distributed, so hopefully you can get your hands on one.

In appreciation of the artists' involvement with the cookbook, some key executives from Crisco came to town for Fan Fair 2004 and hosted a reception for us at the Palm restaurant. The Crisco brand is owned by the J.M. Smucker Company, a company which is headquartered in Orrville, Ohio, and has been family run for four generations. I had the opportunity to meet the company's chief executives, brothers Richard and Timothy Smucker. I was quite impressed by how warm and down-to-earth they seem. I then discovered that the company was recognized as the top company in *Fortune* magazine's 2003 annual survey of The 100 Best Companies to Work For and has ranked consistently in the top twenty-five companies each year since *Fortune* began the list in 1998.

I got a chance to chat for a bit with Mark Wills, Steve Azar, and Rhonda Vincent at the reception. We artists rarely have the chance to get caught up with one another. I have to tell you that it's been my experience that most of my peers in this industry are pretty nice people.

After a couple of hours of active schmoozing, I came

home and visited with everyone. I've got a big day tomorrow. The PaJAMa Party is going to the Crisco booth in the Nashville Convention Center to sign autographs at 10 a.m., and then we've got our Fan Fair concert to do, so it's lights out early tonight.

June 11th

The autograph signing went great. It requires a lot more time, however, when you've got all four of us PaJAMa Party girls signing and then posing for group shots. I wish we could have stayed for a couple of more hours, but we had to get to the show. The PaJAMa Party is a relatively new idea for the fans out there, so it's great to see their reaction when we all hit the stage together. It was a fun show.

I enjoy doing Fan Fair. It gives you a chance to give a little bit of yourself back to the fans, sign an autograph, and take a picture with someone who has supported your music.

I came home and packed because I have to leave tomorrow morning for a couple of PaJAMa Party shows. Tomorrow night we'll be in Nashville, Indiana, and then we're off to Salem, Ohio, for Sunday night.

We had another fun night at home with the family. Everyone will be here until Monday morning, which means, unfortunately, I'm going to miss out on a couple of days with them, but that's the way it goes when you do what I do.

June 12th

I found out this morning that it's the water pump that broke on my car. As a result, the engine is totally fried. I need time to digest this information and decide what I want to do. Do I fix it or get a different car? I'll sort that out when I get home.

You're not going to believe this, either. When I got to the PaJAMa Party tour bus this morning, the air conditioner had just stopped working! For those of you who are counting, that's three air conditioners in four days. Unbelievable!

You simply cannot ride on a tour bus without any air conditioning because usually the bus windows do not open. On some buses you can open a window or two, but even then, forget about it.

We had a bus air conditioner break down once while we were driving through the desert in Arizona. We were on a tight schedule for a show we had to get to, which meant we didn't have time to stop and repair it, so we tried to hold the windows

Photographer: Lise Monpetit

open with hangers while we were doing seventy miles an hour hurrying to get to the show. Our efforts didn't cool the bus down much, but we did make it to the show on time.

We didn't have a lot of spare time to get to this show, either. Raymond Hicks, Deborah Allen's manager and husband, also is the road manager for the PaJAMa Party. He's got a lot of responsibility to make sure we get to the show. He was doing his best to stay calm as we headed to the bus company shop to see if they could fix the air conditioner. He got us a really nice bus for this trip and I know he wants to take good care of us girls, but if they can't fix this it's hard to say what we're going to end up with. This is a really busy time of year for touring, so buses are hard to come by.

We get to the shop and time is tickin' and they can't seem to fix the bus. But they do have another one, thank goodness, and for those of us who've traveled on the road in vans and cars with hardly a floorboard, any bus will do.

Off we go and we arrive at the venue less than an hour and a half before show time. Imagine the scene backstage. There we are, four girls crammed into one dressing room, trying to get ready in a short amount of time. It's quite a sight. There are a few other dressing rooms available; I think it's cute that we girls want to be together.

We did two shows tonight and had a great time. I had a chance to see some American fans that I hadn't seen for a few years. (You can tour America for five years and never play the same place twice.) But the biggest surprise for me tonight was that a group of my Canadian friends and supporters showed up, too.

I really enjoy seeing and visiting with these people who show such love and appreciation for my music. There is a small group of longtime fans that I have come to trust and who have become my friends. Public people tend to become pretty protective of their privacy: there is only so much of yourself you can give, and you don't want to hurt anyone by not having time for them. You have to keep the circle pretty small. But it's been great to see how these folks have become friends with one another other as well. They spend time together throughout the year.

It's midnight and the bus is loaded and ready to roll. I'm in my bunk ready for a good night's sleep. I'm looking forward to tomorrow.

June 13th

We arrived safely at tonight's venue: Ponderosa Park in Salem, Ohio. I slept like a baby on the bus last night. Our driver is really good. And the humming of the bus rolling along put me to sleep pretty quickly. Thank God I can sleep out here on the road. Occasionally, I have a sleepless night, but that doesn't happen too often.

I was looking forward to the show tonight because we were sharing the stage with Lee Roy Parnell and David Lee Murphy. Along with Alan Jackson, Lee Roy and I were the first artists signed to Arista Records when the company opened its Nashville division in 1989. We were three artists with a dream, and it's wonderful to look back and know that dreams do come true. I was just thinking about how Lee Roy, Alan, and I would be out there on the road together along with the president of Arista Nashville, Tim Dubois. We would visit radio stations and introduce ourselves and hope that they would play our records. It was a very exciting time for us and for country music. Seeing Lee Roy again and getting a chance to hear him perform was really great. He's a soulful singer and fine guitar player.

The PaJAMa Party show went very well and it was fun to play Ponderosa Park again. The park had been closed for a few years and only recently reopened.

We signed autographs for a while and then climbed on the bus and headed home. We watched a couple of movies that I've been wanting to see: *Big Fish* and *Monster*. They were very different. *Monster* was so dark and *Big Fish* was so light. I can see why Charlize Theron won the Oscar for her performance in *Monster*. I enjoy Tim Burton's directorial style; *Big Fish* is another example of his unique vision.

Being a part of the PaJAMa Party, with its three different artists and their three very different ways of doing things, has presented some challenges for all of us (which is, I think, inevitable), but I feel confident that as long as we girls keep communicating, we will be able to sort things out. The good thing about our situation is that everyone's heart is in the right place.

I'm used to being in charge. But as a PaJAMa Party member, I'm having to let go of the reins. I'm having to trust that everything is going to be all right. That's hard for me. I'm trying to stay open and learn the lessons I'm here to learn in this situation, but I'm also very protective of my career and image (as we all are), so we have to learn how to accommodate one another.

Raymond was the Oak Ridge Boys' road manager for years. He's used to dealing with the dynamics of four interacting personalities. On the other hand, the other girls are all used to running their own shows, as I am. So we're all on a learning curve in this situation. Some conversations have not been easy as we all speak our minds and express our needs, but there's been a lot of group hugs, too.

All is good, but interestingly enough, I'm having a sleepless night tonight. (And after just having written about how easily I can sleep on the bus.) It seems I have a few things on my mind that I have to think through.

June 14th

I got home at about 6 a.m. Johnny and Mia met me with a smile. They were up playing chess. I'm glad they were awake. Marco was on his way home from dropping off the rest of the family members at the airport. He got back about 7 a.m. We had a nice breakfast together and visited a bit before Johnny and Mia had to be driven to the airport. I'm glad I got to see them before they left. It was a nice way to end the family visit.

Marco and I went car shopping after he returned home

since I decided not to bother with fixing my car because of all the damage that had been done when it had overheated. Car shopping alone is exhausting, but doing it after not getting any sleep in about twenty-four hours is even worse. I was feeling a bit concerned about having so many other things that I needed to do—getting caught up on my journals, finding songs, and getting the house back in order.

Marco asked me to take my time, to avoid being impulsive. He told me to enjoy the process of buying the car. I'm smiling as I'm writing this because the first car that we got into we were both saying, "Wow. This is really nice. Do you want to buy it?"

Three o'clock rolled around. Marco could tell I was getting really tired, so he suggested we go home and relax, get a good night's sleep, and start again tomorrow. That's what we did.

June 15th

We did more car shopping today. It was fun, but I'm not sure which car I want to buy. I don't really think much about cars, but now that I'm looking to buy one I'm noticing everything about them. Marco mentioned that the same thing was happening to him. I didn't see anything I really wanted.

I packed for a show the PaJAMa Party is doing in Minnesota. We leave on the bus tomorrow afternoon.

June 16th

I slept in and it felt so good.

I have been presented with the opportunity to host a country music radio show profiling the women of country music. I think it's a great idea. Brian and I have been talking about it for some time, and now we're moving to the contract negotiation stage with the company that produces the show. We'll see how it goes.

I'm on the bus with all the gang of the PaJAMa Party. It's good to see everyone. We've got a long drive ahead of us. I'm going to take advantage of this and work on my journals.

June 17th

The show was so much fun tonight. We performed on a stage in the middle of a field with a few thousand people ready to party. It's a familiar sight when you're touring in the summertime and doing outdoor music festivals. I love it.

We shared the stage with another group similar to ours. They call themselves the Honky Tonk Tailgate Party, featuring Rhett Akins, Chad Brock, Daryl Singletary, and David Kersh. I hadn't seen these guys for a while, so it was fun to get a chance to say hi and hang out a bit.

We signed autographs, climbed back on the bus, and headed back home. Once again, I took advantage of this time to work on my journals.

June 18th

We got home about 3 p.m. I've had conversations with a few Mercedes dealers and some mechanics that work on foreign cars. One company I spoke with has been in business for thirty years; the owner's father was the head engineer at the Mercedes factory in Germany for twenty-five years. The general consensus is that I should repair my car. After considerable thought, I feel good about it and so does Marco.

I'm all done car shopping now.

June 19th

We went to Centennial Park in Nashville today to an American Artisan Festival to see Jen Cohen, a friend of ours, perform. Jen is moving back to New York soon to become a cantor, that is, prayer leader, in the Jewish faith.

We hooked up with a bunch of our other friends as well and decided that it's time to have a barbecue at someone's house. Thursday night at Bonnie Spence's house. Bonnie is the girlfriend of a good buddy of ours, Joey Britt. He is going to ask her to marry him this weekend. We really like her, so we're excited for him.

Mike, our friend who just got married, told us he just found out that his wife, Trisha, is pregnant. Like all first-time fathers, he's really happy, but scared, too.

It was a great day of fun and take-out food.

June 20th

Got up early and went to church. It's Father's Day, so we laid pretty low. I called my dad and had a nice talk. I always enjoy talking to him. Although at certain points in my life we didn't spend much time together, I like rebuilding our relationship now. He's a really funny guy. I find this interesting because I did spend my early years with him, and his influence appears to be a part of my decisions in life today: Marco is very funny and in that way reminds me of my father.

June 21st

Cleaned house. There is so much laundry to do. Believe it or not, I have just started getting everything back into place after the family visit.

June 22nd

Lots more housework, and I organized some songwriting and song-listening appointments. Eric Silver and his wife, Adele, celebrated their one-year anniversary tonight, so we all gathered at the Sunset Grill for dinner. Marco and I had fun. It was nice to hang with some new people, and to enjoy the company of some of our friends that we haven't seen for a while.

June 23rd

I picked up my godson, Joey, this morning and spent a little bit of time visiting with Red and Bonnie, Joey's grandparents. I told Joey that I want to spend time with him, but today I needed to do as much journaling as I could, and he said, "That's all right, I'll just read." He loves to read. Happily for Joey, Marco decided that the two of them needed to spend some time together. They went to the movies and played some basketball while I worked on my journals. I was happy to see them together because I'm hoping that Joey and Marco will develop a good friendship. I played some basketball, too, and Joey and I sat outside and visited. There's not a lot we have in common, but I can feel it's important to him that we spend time together. It's important to me, and it's nice when

Precious moments with my godson Joey Smith.

that feeling is reciprocated. He's a good kid.

June 24th

Marco is working in Nashville this weekend.

Took Joey back to his dad's house. Worked on my journal.

It's Thursday, so as planned we went to Bonnie Spence's house for a barbecue with some of our friends. We met some new people, too. Marco told me Joey Britt is all set to ask Bonnie to marry him this Saturday. We're excited for them. We'll see if he does it.

June 25th

Journaled all day today.

June 26th

Picked up my godson Joey again today. This was his special day. We did everything he wanted to do. Basically, we spent the day at the pool.

Marco worked today and then requested that we go to church tonight so we don't have to get up and go to the early service of church tomorrow. He has to be at work tomorrow by 10 a.m. I think it's the first time I've gone to the Saturday evening service.

June 27th

Marco got up early for work, and Joey and I slept in. Joey wanted French toast for breakfast. I made it with cinnamon raisin bread and it was delicious. He is leaving early tomorrow morning for a trip to Alabama with his father. They are going to spend a few days at the beach.

I brought him home in the early afternoon and spent the rest of the afternoon shopping and preparing a nice meal for Marco and me. When I got home, Marco told me that Joey Britt had indeed popped the question to Bonnie, and she accepted. We're happy for them both.

June 28th

Worked out, then went to a song-listening meeting at BMG with Michelle Berlin. Debbie Zavitson came to the meeting with me. Debbie is Russ's wife. She works in the industry as an independent A & R ("artist and repertoire") consultant. As they say on Music Row, "she has a good ear for good song." It was my first song meeting with Debbie being on my team. She's found a lot of hit songs for everyone from Blake Shelton to LeAnn Rimes.

Debbie plans to set up a lot of publisher meetings for us, then come along with me, listen to the material presented by the publishers' songpluggers, and share her point of view about the tunes and their merits. Having someone like Debbie helping me to find songs is an integral part of the process of making records here in Nashville. Every artist that doesn't write all of the songs on their albums needs someone like Debbie on their team.

Then we went to Debbie's office and listened to a bunch of songs that I was considering for recording, and she played me a few things that she really likes. It seems that Debbie likes a lot of the same songs that I like, so the day went smoothly. Plus it's nice to have another woman's perspective on the material.

June 29th

I spent all morning at home listening to songs, and then Debbie and I went to a meeting with Terry Wakefield at Sony Music Publishing this afternoon to hear some more material. Terry worked at Arista Records when I was signed there. I hadn't seen him in a few years. It was nice to visit with him, and he played us some really good songs. One that caught my ear is called "My Give a Damn's Busted." I think it's funny. It expresses an emotion and a truth that we've all experienced at times in our lives.

June 30th

Went to Universal to listen to songs and then went to a Chicks with Hits meeting. I didn't hear anything that really caught my ear. I'm thinking about recording a song the Chicks played me some time ago. It's called "Like an Angel." It's a favorite of the Chicks. I really like it, too. It's a girl song.

Marco left for Texas.

July 1st

It's my birthday. I got a beautiful stainless steel barbecue as my gift. It's exactly what I wanted. Marco thinks it's great that I ask for such practical gifts, but he's concerned that people will think he's not very romantic with his gift giving, which is so far from the truth. I wanted a barbecue and that's what I got.

Since Marco is in Texas for my birthday, he went and picked up the barbecue before he left. They had run out of the model I wanted, but they had a floor model already assembled. He called me and asked me if I would want that. Of course I said yes, because that meant we wouldn't have to put it together. He loaded it up in the van and headed home, but took a corner too quickly and the barbecue went flying. Marco was so upset. He thought he had destroyed it. But there were only a couple of dents in places that aren't visible. It's a beautiful barbecue and we're going to have a lot of fun cooking and having parties out on the deck.

I had a music -listening meeting with Tony and Russ today. My manager, Brian, was also there. He had a beautiful bouquet of flowers delivered to the meeting for my birthday. That was very thoughtful. We started the meeting at 9 a.m. and finished up around 3 p.m. It was great to hang out with the guys and listen to songs. We are on the same page, musically. I'm feeling really good about everything.

July 2nd

I wrote with Darryl Burgess and Cyril Rawson today. We finished "Rose Colored Sky." I like it. I thought it would only take a few hours to complete, but it took all day. We just had a few lines to finish, but it was challenging to find the right words. Darryl and Cyril are two fine young Canadians that I've known for years. I've written more with Cyril than I have with Darryl. It would be great if we had a hit together.

The PaJAMa Party is doing a venue in Georgia called The Swallow at the Hollow soon. It's a venue that features songwriters, so I am going to add a few more songs that I've written to the show. Ed Smoak, one of the guitar players for the PaJAMa party, is going to accompany us. He came to the house tonight and we rehearsed the new songs I plan to do. Ed is such a nice guy, and a great guitar player. It'll be a fun gig.

July 3rd

I spent all day cleaning Marco's car. Can you believe that? I also bought him new seat covers and car mats. You see, I am using his car while my car is in the shop. Mercedes did offer me a loaner, but my car should be ready any day now, so I'll just keep driving Marco's. But it definitely needed a cleaning. I'm doing it to surprise him. Marco uses this car like a truck; it was in serious need of a cleaning. I think he's going to like it. He's a very neat and tidy guy (or at least he's been putting up a good front for me since we've been married), but the car was another story.

I laid low this evening. Marco is having a good show in Texas. All is well.

July 4th

I worked outside and spent several hours journaling. Since Marco is out of town, this is a good time for me to take advantage of my time alone. It's been a nice, peaceful day.

July 5th

Marco came home tonight. I took care of some business around the house, did some grocery shopping, and prepared a nice meal. Absence does make the heart grow fonder. The house is so much more alive when Marco comes home. Life is good.

July 6th

I had a music meeting with Tony and Russ today from 9 a.m. to 3:30 p.m. We heard some good songs and agreed on a few.

Then I went to the gym. I lost some pounds last month, but I've been putting a few back on. I have to make more time for working out. This is where I'm losing the battle; I'm eating pretty well, but I just have to get to the gym more often. I think I may have to start using my treadmill in our workout room upstairs. I'm trying to make time for Marco and me to go to the gym together because I know it's something he wants us to do, but getting each other on the same schedule is part of the problem. He likes to get up around 6 a.m., and I'm not ready to face the day until 8 a.m. In fact, after years of being on the road and working nights, I'm definitely not a morning person. We've discussed adding a couple more machines to our home workout room so that we could work out together up there. We currently have weights and the treadmill.

July 7th

I had another music meeting from 9 a.m. until 2:30 p.m. today with Russ and Tony. It's amazing how much time this process can take. But it's understandable, I guess: we're listening to a lot of material—dozens of songs at each listening session, hundreds of songs altogether. We're trying to find that needle in the haystack—a song with that magical something that makes us love it and want to record it.

I'm going to hang out with my godson Joey tonight. His summer visit with his father in Nashville has almost come to an end. He's leaving on the 11th to go home to his mom in Wyoming, so this is the last chance I have to see him. I wish he lived in Nashville. We just started getting to know each other and then it's time for him to go again. He only comes to Nashville once a year, during the summer, which is often the busiest time for me. I'm trying to make as much time for him as I can (I find myself feeling guilty because I wonder if I'm making enough time for him). I want him to know that he really matters to me. It's times like these that make me wonder about having a child—there just does not seem to be enough hours in a day.

July 8th

Joey and I went to the pool. He played with the kids. I listened to some songs and brought my laptop with me to do some journaling. After a little while, Joey came to me and said, "Aunt Michelle, can you not work today and just play with me?" So I spent the rest of the day hanging with my godson and not working. We swam in the pool, played basketball, and had a barbecue. In the evening we played cards. He's a really smart kid and it's nice getting to know him.

The PaJAMa party is playing tomorrow night at The Swallow at the Hollow in Roswell, Georgia, and we're all driving ourselves there. My car is not ready yet, so Mercedes is going to give me a loaner. I have to pick it up tomorrow morning. I'm looking forward to the drive. I'll be able to listen to more songs and I always enjoy jumping in the car and just driving.

I'm packed and ready to go away for the weekend.

July 9th

I brought Joey back to his dad's this morning and picked up the loaner from Mercedes.

The trip to Roswell took longer than expected—about five hours—but we all got there eventually, did a sound check, and grabbed something to eat. As we were eating, we noticed that all the Swallow at the Hollow staff were wearing pajamas. We thought that was cute. Then they started to ask us what kind of pajamas we were going to wear. Hmm...It seems the club's owner had advertised we'll be performing in our pajamas! Not something we normally do, but we're finding that people are taking the "pajama party" title quite literally. Apparently, the club owner has advertised that anyone who arrives in their pajamas would get a free drink. It's all in good fun, but the Kinleys didn't bring appropriate pajama-wear, so they had to make a Wal-Mart run. Deborah and I happened to bring something that we could wear, so we were fine. It was fun and we had a good night. We literally had a "pajama party" in Roswell!

July 10th

We don't often get a chance to stay in one place for two nights, but since this is a two-day gig we stayed up late last night and hung out together until 3:30 a.m. It was a lot of fun.

We have a lot to learn about each other. Deborah Allen shared some of her journey as an artist. What an incredible career she's had. She's a real go-getter and very creative. She's an inspiration.

I slept in this morning, worked out, and later went for dinner with the gang. Deborah had gone shopping for another pair of pajamas to wear to tonight's show. Then I decided I needed to get a different pair as well. Deborah went shopping with me, but we couldn't find anything I liked. It's a good thing she found another pair of pajamas to wear because, as we were getting ready for the show, I was ironing mine and I burnt a big hole in the top! That left me without any pajamas to wear, but Deborah let me borrow the ones she had worn last night. There are definite advantages to having other women out here on the road. We share lipstick, shoes, and hair and makeup tips. And pajamas, if necessary. It's great.

The shows were a lot of fun and, I think, a good bonding experience for us girls.

July 11th

We stayed up too late again last night, but I got up around 9 a.m. and headed home. It was a pleasant drive and I'm glad to be home with my family. We had a barbecue and a quiet night.

July 12th

I went to the gym this morning. I'm continuing to fight the good fight.

I had another music meeting with Tony and Russ this afternoon. We are going into the studio in one week. I'm pretty excited. I feel like we have some really good songs. We are going to record the basic instrumental tracks (the "bed tracks") for my Christmas album next Monday and Tuesday. We expect to record six songs each day. Then on Wednesday we are going to record six tracks for my country CD.

In the record business we call the process of recording the basic musical components of a song "cutting the bed track."

Generally, when we "cut a bed" we have the drummer, bassist, electric guitarist, acoustic guitarist, keyboardist, and steel/dobro player record a song's basic elements without any instrumental solos or vocal parts. I'll be in the studio, too, singing what we call a "ghost vocal," which everyone can hear and use as a musical reference. Hopefully, my singing will inspire the players and give them a sense of the energy and the musical attitude I'm looking for in the song. During this time we also find the right tempo for the performance and the right key in which the song should be performed. It's a very creative process, with everyone participating, offering suggestions and ideas. The whole process, however, is always overseen by my producers—in this case, Tony and Russ—who make sure the results of the recording are true to both our collective vision for the song and our overall concept for the entire album.

We were going to record on Thursday as well, but have decided to look for more songs and get back into the studio as soon as we find a couple more that we love. We have eight songs for my country CD, maybe even ten, so we really only need two more.

I feel relaxed and confident about the approach we're taking with these albums. I really like Russ and Tony and I enjoy the energy that we have together. I look forward to getting into the studio with them.

July 13th

I went to the gym today and worked on my journals. I'm a bit behind, so I have some catching up to do. I haven't turned in my installment for April, May, and June, but I'm close to getting it done, and then I need to get caught up on July. Oh...I'm so back in school again.

July 14th

Gym and journals. That's it.

July 15ᵗʰ

I did some voice-over work for some commercials for TSC this morning. Then I went to the gym. After that, Marco and I went to the movies. We saw *The Day After Tomorrow*, starring Dennis Quaid. The special effects were great. The thought of Earth being destroyed by another ice age is not a pleasant thought, but it was still a good movie with lots of suspense.

The PaJAMa Party is flying to Pierce, Nebraska early tomorrow morning, so I'm packed and ready to go. I have to get up at 4 a.m. and it's midnight, so I'd better call it a day. Goodnight.

July 16ᵗʰ

Oh my, what a long day. Days like this deepen my appreciation of traveling by tour bus. This run went flawlessly, but it was pretty grueling.

I got up at 4 a.m. for a 5:30 a.m. airport call. Two flights later and we were in Omaha, Nebraska. Since this was a fly-in date, we rented a couple of vans and checked into a hotel in Omaha for a couple of hours of down time. We all had lunch, got our clothes ready for the show, and loaded up in the vans for a three-hour drive to Pierce, where we performed at the county fair. The show went great. We signed autographs afterwards, loaded up the vans once again, and drove another three hours back to the hotel in Omaha, arriving at about 3 a.m. Exhausted is the only word I can use. I'm going to sleep for a couple of hours. We have a 5:30 a.m. lobby call tomorrow morning for the flights home. Love the Biz!

July 17ᵗʰ

Well, everyone was pretty much draggin' their butts this morning, but we all made it home safe and sound. It's 5:30 in the afternoon and I'm going to bed.

I slept until 8 a.m. Marco and I went to church. The sermon today focused on dealing with pain, disappointment, and loss in our lives. That is the human condition, no matter who you are. The underlying message of the service was that most people who lean on God during these challenging times seem to find comfort.

It has been my experience that when I'm feeling challenged I know I'm not alone, and I trust all things happen for a reason. I'm not feeling a lot of stress or challenge right now, even though I'm in the middle of making a record. I feel at peace. I believe that all things are as they should be.

At our church, as with most churches, we are a community of fellowship. We help each other out if someone has lost a loved one or if a marriage is going through a rough time. The pastor and his wife are there for you, if you need to talk. Today, Pastor Foster was encouraging us to be open with our feelings. For example, if some folks at church ask you how you're doing and if you're not doing all that well, why don't you say that you're going through a tough time as opposed to saying you're fine? Maybe they'll ask you to go for a coffee or get a group of people together to go out and have some fun. When I was going through a really difficult time a few years ago, my friends rallied around me and helped to keep me busy and made sure we had some parties together and hung out with each other. We talked and laughed and I didn't feel alone. It's important to know that you're not alone and that it's OK to reach out and ask for help.

I understand how pride can keep us from wanting anyone to know that we are having a hard time. Somehow we've been taught as a society that if you're facing difficulty, then you must not have your act together. Showing weakness or vulnerability is so hard for some of us, especially in the male-dominated industry I work in. But I like it when people show their imperfections because then I don't have to pretend that I'm perfect. It's a function of the human condition that we are all going to have some hard times; if you can work through the challenges with some fellowship and support, not only will you build deeper relationships but the lessons learned will be invaluable. I know that there are people out there who are alone and don't have family to depend on. I believe that if you see someone in need that you should lend an ear or ask if there is anything you can do to help—without getting tangled up in someone's life, but just to give a few minutes of your time for support or some words of encouragement.

Coincidentally, after the service I ran into a fellow musician that I hadn't seen for a long while. I asked him how he was doing because I knew he had been planning to get married. We sat down and talked. He told me that the marriage didn't happen and that he was feeling a great deal of sadness, feeling really alone. I told him I believed that all things happen as they should. As we talked, he told me that he was having second thoughts about getting married anyhow because something just didn't seem right between him and his fiancée. He knew he had to remember that it was better for him in the long run that they didn't get married. I consider marriage a pretty serious commitment: if there are strong feelings of doubt, then getting married is not going to change that. This person is just so ready to have a family and share his life with someone. I think ultimately that's what most of us want. I can't wait until he tells me that he's found "the right one." He's a very sweet guy and I believe the right one is out there for him. The right one is out there for all of us. You just have to be patient and follow your heart and your intuition and you will make the right choice.

I believe the right choice is based on how that person treats you. Do you feel safe, loved, and valued when you're together? Can you talk deeply to each other? Do you feel respect? Do you share common spiritual beliefs, and do you have common goals? Can you be yourself, warts and all? I think a sense of humor is really important, too. Also, you really have to like this person as a friend, because you are going to be spending a large percentage of your life doing everyday mundane things together, and if you can have a good time doing them, then that's another good sign.

After church, Marco and I went to visit Pat and Celeste. We took them out for brunch and then went back and visited at their house well into the evening. They are both starting the infamous ten-day fast tomorrow, so we blew it out with food and beverages. These are two of my favorite people in the world.

We start recording tomorrow morning at 10 a.m. I'm pretty excited. It will be pretend-Christmas for the next couple of days. I'd better get some sleep.

July 19th

We had a great time in the studio today. Jamie O'Neal, a singer/songwriter who had the big hit "There Is No Arizona," is married to Rodney Good, a recording engineer. They have a fully-equipped recording studio built on the lower level of their home. They call it The Grotto. It's a comfortable and relaxing place to make music.

Russ's wife, Debbie, was kind enough to bring us a Christmas tree so we could have a little holiday vibe going on in the studio. Christmas in July. I thought it would be hard to get into the mood, but Christmas music has a way of making you feel good, so it's not difficult at all.

We had three recording sessions today. One at 10 a.m., one at 2 p.m., and another at 6 p.m. We recorded six tunes today including, "Rudolph the Red Nosed Reindeer," "Jingle Bell Rock," "Little Drummer Boy," "Go Tell It on the Mountain," "Silent Night," and a new song written by my pal Patricia Conroy, "I Know Santa's Been Here." We're right on schedule. I'm very happy with the musical arrangements we've developed. Some are very traditional, while others are quite different from the original Christmas recordings. And the band rocks!

I've worked with most of these musicians over the years.

It was good to see everyone again. We always take a lunch break during recording, and it was nice to get caught up with everyone then. The band consists of the session leader, John Willis, on lead guitar and slide guitar; Jerry Kimbrough on acoustic guitar and mandolin; Joe Chemay on bass guitar; Catherine Styron Marx on keyboards; Wane Killius on drums; and Dan Dugmore on dobro and steel guitar.

We left the studio feeling really positive. It's been a good day's work.

I'm pretty tired now, so I'm going to shut it down and start again tomorrow.

My producers, Tony Hazeldon and Russ Zavitson, in the studio with bass player/background vocalist extraordinaire Joe Chemay (seated).

July 20th

Today was another day with three sessions. Another 10, 2, and 6. We remain on schedule with another six tracks recorded: "Joy to the World," "White Christmas," "O Come All Ye Faithful", "Winter Wonderland," "Christmas Song," and "Have Yourself a Merry Little Christmas." That means we're finished with all twelve bed tracks for the Christmas CD. Yeah!

A new keyboard player joined us for these sessions. His name is Gordon Mote, and he is an incredible musician. I feel magic when I hear him play. Gordon is blind, and it's amazing when you consider how he responded to that reality in his life by becoming one of the best session pianists with whom I have had the privilege to work, and currently one of the fastest-rising studio musicians in Nashville. He was recording with Martina McBride yesterday so he was unable to join us until today.

I'm so excited about the arrangements we came up with these past two days. I wanted to record a Christmas CD that had some traditional values in the recordings as well as a few creative approaches to the arrangements and I feel like we have accomplished both. I particularly like our version of "White Christmas," a very sparse and elegant arrangement with Gordon accompanying me on solo piano. I also really love "Joy to the World."

There's a lot more work to be done on the Christmas CD, but tomorrow we're going to record six bed tracks for my next country record. I can't wait. It's been several years since I've been in the studio to record a country CD.

Once again, I'm going to bring a contemporary approach to the music. I'm not a traditional country artist in the strict sense of the word. But I grew up singing country, and I've been singing country all my life, so there will always be some traditional country influences in my music.

July 21st

We did another 10, 2, and 6 today. We recorded six tracks for my country CD and I couldn't be happier. I love the energy and the edge and the groove of this record. The songs we recorded today are "You Can't Lose Them All," "I've Forgotten You," "Something Wild," "My Give a Damn's Busted," "Voodoo," and "I Don't Want To Be That Strong."

I'm having a great time, and I can't wait to get in and record my keeper vocals.

July 22nd

I had a hair appointment this morning and a full rehearsal with my band this afternoon. It was great to see the guys and to play some music with them. I know I say that every time I get together with my band, but I really mean it. We're friends and we enjoy hangin' together.

I came home after rehearsal at about 6 p.m. and Marco had everything ready to go for a nice dinner. We had salad, salmon, and broccoli and zucchini from the garden. How nice is that! After dinner I packed for a 12 a.m. departure with the PaJAMa Party. We are heading out for a show tomorrow night in Indiana. Then Brad and I are going to hook up with my band to do a show in Chapleau, Ontario, the following evening. My band will leave Nashville in another bus tomorrow afternoon, and, if all goes as planned, Brad and I will get off the one bus and jump onto the other at a specific time. My fingers are crossed that the plan will work out okay. I can't see any reason why it won't—unless something unexpected happens. Of course, I have learned to expect the unexpected, but I'm going to stay positive.

I'm on the PaJAMa Party bus now. It's great to see everyone, but it's late and we're all climbing into our bunks (except the driver, of course). Down the road we go.

July 23rd

We arrived safely in La Porte, Indiana, and had a great show tonight. The girls and I were talking about how much we enjoy doing this show together and sharing the load.

The Kinleys have a new single out called "Little Shoulders." It's a really good song about a mother and father contemplating divorce, but they're asking themselves if they really want to put the weight of a broken family onto the little shoulders of their children. That's a powerful thought. I hope it does well for them. It's a different time right now in country music and it's not easy to get a record on the radio. It's always been challenging, but I think it's even tougher now.

It takes a lot of money to market artists to radio these days.

I kept in touch with my band throughout the day. They left Nashville on time. Everything seems to be on track. I'll hook up with them at about 2:30 a.m.

July 24th

The plan worked well. Brad and I met up with our bus at 2:45 a.m. and we headed up to Chapleau, six hundred miles further north. We arrived safe, sound, and on time. Once again we had another fun show. The audience was great and I signed a lot of autographs. As the bus was being loaded, the northern lights started dancing. They were so beautiful, and they continued to dance as we headed down the highway. We pulled over and tried to get pictures, but none of our cameras were sufficiently high tech to capture the spectacle.

I'm feeling a cold coming on. That makes me a bit nervous because I have to sing in the studio in a couple of days. Maybe I'm worn down from the traveling and late nights, so I'll just get a good night's sleep tonight.

July 25th

I got lots of sleep last night. And, as I'm typing this, I'm happy to report that I'm caught up on my journals, too. Now if I could just get all my closets organized! How obsessive am I? I was hoping to get this done and on track because I start in the studio tomorrow and will be spending a lot of time recording over the next few weeks. I just spoke to Marco and we are going to have pizza for dinner tonight and hang with each other before I disappear into the studio. We start recording my vocals for the Christmas record first.

July 26th

Recording the vocals went great today. I love to sing and it's a privilege to be able to make records. I'm having a great time working with Tony and Russ. It's fantastic.

I've decided that I want to do the syndicated radio show

that has been offered to me. I read one of the scripts the radio people are suggesting for the show and I really like the writing. It feels relaxed and real. Now I need to record a demo of the program. It's going to be a sixty-minute weekly show, syndicated internationally. We're going to call it *The Women of Country with Michelle Wright*. I'm not sure when I'm going to be able to get the demo done, but I'm looking forward to doing it.

July 27th

Recorded more vocals today. Once again, we had a great time and we're getting a lot done. I'm surprised at how smoothly it's going. I thought these Christmas vocals may have been more challenging than a regular record, but so far so good. How fun.

July 28th

Marco left for Texas today. I stayed home and cleaned house and listened to more material for my country CD. We had planned to record the demo reel for the radio show this morning, but I really needed to have this day off so I could get caught up on a few things around the house. I've learned to stay connected to the fact that I need to have a day off every week, and since I'm going out on the road this weekend, I need to use this day for other things. It's hard to say no, but I'm learning.

July 29th

We recorded more vocals today. We're almost finished.

July 30th

Finished the vocals for the Christmas record. Now we have to record the harmony vocals and all the instrumental overdubs such as the strings, the jingle bell sounds, and all the effects that will make this CD sound like a Christmas record. I also want to put fiddle on some of the songs. We haven't decided which tunes should have fiddle, but I know Russ and Tony have some good ideas.

We're going to talk about the arrangements and make some final decisions. I want the listener to be taken on a journey with a nice variety of sounds and ideas. I feel we've accomplished that.

The band and I are off to Atlantic Canada tomorrow, to the province of Newfoundland for a concert in St. John's, the capital city. I'm particularly looking forward to this trip. I enjoy having the opportunity to experience the wonderful people of Newfoundland. It's hard to explain, but the people there are very warm and friendly and welcoming. It's almost like entering a different country, and I think it's safe to say that because they live on "the rock," their island life experience is somewhat different from those of us who live on a much larger land mass. I think they really have to depend on each other. I'd recommend a trip to Newfoundland any day.

July 31st

Getting to Newfoundland proved to be much more of a challenge than we had anticipated. Our flight was delayed fifty minutes out of Nashville to Toronto. This put us at risk of missing our connection to Newfoundland, and all of the flights from Toronto to St. John's for the following day were sold out. And whenever we come in from Nashville to any airport in Canada we have a border crossing to contend with, so I was starting to feel pretty concerned about whether or not we were going to be able to make it to the show. We finally boarded the flight in Nashville, and, thanks to Air Canada in Toronto, we did manage to catch our connecting flight. Air Canada's concierge staff had a van ready to take us to the next terminal as soon as we landed in Toronto. It was quite a sight. We ran through the airport as fast as we could while our equipment was being transferred and inspected by Canada Customs. We landed in Newfoundland at 3:30 a.m. All our gear and luggage arrived, too. That was a close call. We all were exhausted, but happy to be in St. John's.

The driver who picked us up was really friendly. He told us he had never been off "the rock." To those of us who have traveled around the world that is almost unimaginable, but he has his family and friends there and feels no need to go anywhere else.

August 1ˢᵗ

We had such a great show tonight. It was an outdoor street festival right on the waterfront in downtown St. John's. There were about six thousand people there. Jimmy Rankin started the show off and the crowd was just rockin'. Once we started our set the audience seemed even more pumped and they sang along to every song and danced and partied. When the energy is high and the crowd has come to have a great time, there is nothing like it. It really is a team effort. We do our part, the audience does their part, and it's magic.

Rockin' with my guitar players, Lee Warren and Sean Smith.
Photographer: Julie Smith

There is a noticeable difference in the vibe of an outdoor show or a large arena. When we are doing an outdoor festival or a large indoor venue the audience tends to be less inhibited than when we are in a smaller theater, which is more intimate and where people tend to be more reserved because they don't want to draw attention to themselves. Once I was able to sort that out I learned to enjoy the variety of venues in which I get to perform.

August 2nd–6th

Our flights home were uneventful, and basically I've been working in the studio recording vocals for the last five days. There's not much to report. All is well. Recording the Christmas CD is much more satisfying than I had expected. Russ and I have been doing a bit of work together without Tony as he's been busy with some previous commitments. It's been fun for me to be able to work one-on-one with Russ and get to know him more. I enjoy these guys, their characters, their work ethics, their humor. I'm a lucky girl. I'm surrounded by a group of men for whom I have a great deal of respect—my husband, my manager, my band members, and now my producers, Russ and Tony. Life is good.

I've tried to tape my radio show demo on my own at home because I have the technology there. But I'm finding it hard to be objective about how I sound. I've asked Brian to book some time in a studio, and I'm going to get his input to help me record the demo.

August 7th

A day off (sort of). Yeah! I just hung out, worked around the house, and did a few things in the yard. It was a nice day.

August 8th

Today was a really special day for Marco and me. We participated in our first Habitat for Humanity homebuilding project. Our church was sponsoring it, so we decided to get involved. Building a home was a great experience. We were able to meet the woman who is going to be the proud owner of the house. We also learned that these people work very hard not only on their own home but also on the homes of other recipients.

I wore my pink leather tool belt that TSC made for me and it was a big hit. We may have to get these into the stores.

A special day: our first Habitat for Humanity homebuilding project.

August 9th

I did a few phone interviews today to promote some shows we're doing in Ontario later this month.

Marco has gone to the doctor today for his physical. It is not something that he has made a priority in his life, but he recognizes that it's important to me, so he's making it a regular part of his life. In talking with other women, I have learned it is not uncommon for men to have to be pushed a little bit harder when it comes to visiting the doctor.

August 10th

I shopped for stage wardrobe the entire day. That's about the best workout you can get. I need a trip to Toronto or New York because I'm having a really hard time finding something unique for the stage. Oh well, I'll just have to make that happen. I've got a photo shoot coming up for the Christmas CD in Toronto, so maybe I'll have time then.

We are leaving at noon tomorrow for four shows with the PaJAMa Party. We will be doing a county fair in Rhode Island and then three shows for the military at bases along the eastern seaboard. I'm really looking forward to the run. I better get packed up.

August 11th

We loaded up the bus and off we went. We girls spent some time getting caught up and then I spent time logging my journals. Being on the tour bus always provides a great opportunity to do some computer work because there is usually nothing to distract me.

The debate is back on about Marco and me having a baby. I cannot believe how deeply concerned we are about this decision. We're just having second thoughts about not having a family and sharing our love and joy. I get a smile on my face when I imagine a miniature Marco running around the house. But I recognize this is not a decision to be taken lightly. I guess I've gone through all the reasons and concerns in past entries, but certainly the biggest ones are that we both travel and we're both in our mid-forties. Will we have the energy that's required?

I've been spending time with the Kinleys on the road and they each have a child and can't recommend it enough. But, the difference is that their husbands don't travel for a living. When I was recording at The Grotto, Jamie O'Neal told me that having a child is the best thing she has ever done. I've started taking prenatal vitamins and we'll see how we're feeling in a couple of months.

Marco and I are thinking about buying some properties in Nashville to enable him to travel less. I have faith that we will make the right decision.

The prayers continue.

August 12th

Russ and Tony are putting background vocals on the Christmas CD today. I wish I could be there, but I'm glad to be out here doing shows. Kim Parent and Joe Chemay are singing the background vocals. They are both really good, so I know their harmonies are going to sound wonderful.

Our show tonight was in Wyoming, Rhode Island. I haven't played New England in a while, so it was nice to meet with my long-time fans there. A few of them brought me pictures from the last time I played this fair.

We were supposed to do two shows, but our second performance got rained out. When we came out onstage for the second show, the rain was just pouring down. Still, there were fans sitting in their chairs under their umbrellas, waiting patiently, showing their support. It was really amazing to see them out there. Unfortunately, we had to stop the concert because it was getting too dangerous to continue. A few people were quite upset that we had to stop, but I've never seen it rain so hard. Of course, we wanted to keep going, but the promoter was concerned about the lightning and the rain. She was right. Water and electricity are not a good combination.

So we're here in Rhode Island dealing with the effects of Hurricane Charlie, which, at this point, has already caused billions of dollars of damage in Florida. Everyone is concerned about what effect the storm's northward progress may have on our shows at the military bases in Hampton, Virginia and Jacksonville, North Carolina. There is literally two feet of water outside the bus right now. Some fairground staff are trying to unplug the water drains. They seem to be having success since the water is starting to go down. Our crew can't load our gear under the bus, however, until the rain lets up, because the equipment could get damaged. We're stuck here for a while, at least.

After a couple of hours of sitting and waiting, we're rolling down the highway en route to the naval base in Groton, Connecticut. Tomorrow we're going to be given a tour of the USS Memphis nuclear submarine. That should be very interesting.

I'm going to get a good night's sleep. Tomorrow will be a full day.

August 13th

Tony and Russ are doing over-dubs on the Christmas CD today. They're putting strings on some songs and adding a few more guitar parts. I can't wait to hear what they've done.

We arrived in Groton safe and sound. The rain had stopped, and it was quite a beautiful day.

Our tour of the submarine was really fascinating. Meeting the senior officers was very impressive. These men showed a confidence and authority that commanded respect. The young sailors were all so respectful and disciplined, too. I noticed that a keen sense of humor seems to exist between the officers and the younger sailors.

Everyone sleeps in bunks not unlike our bunks on the tour bus. But when their craft leaves port, it usually stays out for six months at a time. It's apparent from the conversations I had that these men become a family; they care a lot about one another and watch out for each other.

After touring the USS Memphis, we ate dinner and did the show. It was a lot of fun and the sailors were certainly appreciative. What a great combination! Four girls on stage and a bunch of sailors in the audience!

After the show we learned that tomorrow's concert at Langley Air Force Base in Hampton, Virginia, has been cancelled as a result of Hurricane Charlie's course up the Atlantic coast. There is concern about our next show in Jacksonville, North Carolina, as well, since the eye of the storm is apparently headed in that direction. This news is a real disappointment. Hopefully, the storm will subside. It's done so much damage. I'm hoping the people who are being affected have been able to protect themselves. The news reports don't look good as far as property damage is concerned. We are going to try to drive away from the storm and find a central location that is somewhere between North Carolina and Nashville so that if the show is cancelled we can head back to Tennessee.

August 14th

The show is on for North Carolina tomorrow. But tonight, due to a cancellation, we have the night off. Earlier in the day we drove to a mall in Roanoke, North Carolina. While the guys played golf, the girls went shopping. We all went our separate ways when the four of us hit the stores because we all had different needs. Then, after meeting for dinner at the Olive Garden, we headed back to the bus and showed each other what we had bought. It was a lot of fun.

Right now, the bus is rolling down the highway, and we're on our way to North Carolina.

August 15th

We got to Jacksonville safely, but Hurricane Charlie continues to wreak havoc. The show is being moved indoors into a smaller venue. At least we are going to be able to do the show. They put us up in the officers' quarters. My room is very nice, which I'm happy about. It's like a small apartment. I'm glad to know that the men who are protecting us have a decent place to call home at the end of the day.

There was a nice lunch prepared for us. When we arrived at the mess hall to eat, a wedding was going on, so we had to be quiet. It seems that the couple involved had attempted to get married about a year ago, but another hurricane had come through at the time and their ceremony had to be cancelled. Then he was deployed, so they had to postpone the wedding until his return. Now he's back, they've picked another date, and here they are, once again dealing with a hurricane!

Fortunately, this time they've decided to move the event indoors. I'm happy to announce that the marriage took place (but I do hope that this is not a sign of things to come).

The show went great and the people were so good to us. It really has been a privilege to meet these young men and women who are prepared to give their lives for our safety. It actually moved me to tears a time or two. I'm really thankful for their service. As much as I'd like to see the world living in peace, I'm afraid that is wishful thinking—there are always going to be people wanting to attack others, and we have to be defended.

August 16th

We recorded the demo today for the proposed *Women of Country* radio show. The demo profiled Reba McEntire, Faith Hill, and Terri Clark, and included a "Woman to Watch For" segment with the spotlight on Julie Roberts. We did it at Russ's studio. It was nice to have Russ engineering and Brian giving me perspective. We took several hours to get it done, longer than I thought it would take, but it was the demo reel and my first time doing it. It's important that it be right. I imagine that once I get used to recording the show, it won't take us as long.

August 17th

We continued to put background vocals on the record today. A confession: I do not hear harmonies very well. It's been one of my goals to train my ear to hear them, but since I've always been the lead vocalist, it's not something I ever had to learn. I have tremendous respect for singers who are able to hear harmonies.

I came to the studio today to listen to the background vocals as they were being sung by Kim Parent and Joe Chemay. Things are coming along nicely. Kim is a wonderful lead vocalist in her own right. She's just finished her own album, and she had a copy for me. I'm looking forward to hearing it. We went to lunch together and had a chance to get caught up.

I'm leaving for a concert in Canada tomorrow. I needed to find a special outfit to wear for the show, so after my visit to the studio, I went shopping. I went to one of the more exclusive stores in town, Jamie's. This store brings in a lot of the top designers' clothing. It carries some really beautiful and unique outfits—but you also pay the price. I'm a very frugal person, so I try to shop around at some of the other stores to see if I can find something I like. Then I'll go to Jamie's for a few pieces here and there. Today I found two beautiful blouses that will be perfect for stage. I'm so relieved, because I've been looking around for a while now.

August 18th

More background vocals for the Christmas album today. Another productive day in the studio.

It's just about midnight and we're on the tour bus, headed for a date in London, Ontario. On this run, Paul Hollowell, the PaJAMA Party's keyboard player, is filling in for Dan, our keyboardist. It's good having him out here with us. He's a great musician and a really fun guy to have around. I hope he enjoys himself.

I've made a decision today. This has not been easy for me, but I've decided that I can't continue on with the PaJAMa Party. I'm feeling overwhelmed these days. I'm really excited about everything that's going on in my life—from this book to the radio show to the two new album projects and my upcoming Christmas tour. But all this requires so much of my time and attention that I'm not as available as I need to be for the PaJAMa Party. I think it's only fair to Deborah and the Kinleys that I give them enough notice so they can find a replacement who can be much more available. I'll have to call everyone and I'm not looking forward to that, but I know it's the right thing to do.

August 19th

The show in London went great. Paul did a fine job for us. We played in a beautiful theater, the Grand Theatre, and the crowd was great. I've had the good fortune of having many hit records, and it's so much fun to see the audience singing along, song after song. How different it is now as opposed to when I first started my career. Back then, the audience wasn't very familiar with my music. I used to wonder what it would be like to have a show full of songs that people knew. Now I experience that, and it's very gratifying.

We're staying in London tonight. Our next show is in two days' time, so we'll be driving tomorrow.

August 20th

We drove to Toronto today so that I could meet with the photographer and the stylist who will be working with me on the photo shoot for my Christmas CD. I like them both, and I love the clothes the stylist has found for me to wear. The look is very classic and simple—exactly what I like. We did a fitting and had further discussions about the concept for the photo shoot. I'm always a little nervous about these things because you never know how they will turn out. I'm hoping Laura Szucs, my favorite makeup artist, will be available for the shoot, and I hope that my gut feeling about the direction of the shoot is correct. We'll have to see.

After the meeting I met up with my band and the bus, and now we're driving east to the small town of South Mountain, Ontario. Small towns are always fun to play.

August 22nd

The show went well on the 21. Then we had a long uneventful drive back to Nashville, arriving in Music City at about 4:30 this morning. As always, it's good to be home. But as they say, "there's no rest for the wicked": I'm leaving again tomorrow evening and flying to Winnipeg to participate in a child sponsorship drive for World Vision.

I've got a lot to do before I leave. Mostly household duties. I wish Marco were here, but when he comes home in a couple of days, at least the house will be nice and clean for him. (When he's not here, however, it does allow me to focus on a few things I otherwise might not finish.)

August 23rd

I got a lot done last night. I stayed up late, took care of some office work, and cleaned upstairs.

I dropped Gracie off at the kennel. She is going to be there for a week. That's a long time, but I know she's safe. This is a busy time for Marco and me, so Gracie will be spending a bit more time at the kennel than usual. But they take good care of her and she always looks skinnier when I pick her up. Marco and I give her too many treats.

There were quite a few plane delays en route to Manitoba, and when I finally arrived in Winnipeg, my luggage was delayed coming off the plane. I'm always glad when I arrive safe and sound, and I did eventually get my luggage—it just took them about a half hour to get it to me. I try to remind myself that after having been to Africa and Honduras I shouldn't sweat the small stuff. A few delays here and there don't really matter.

When I finally got my luggage and walked into the airport reception area, it was great to see the World Vision people standing there. A few of the people who traveled with me to Honduras were there, and when you share an experience like that with someone, you become connected in a way that somehow differs from the ordinary. All of us had come in from different parts of North America at around the same time, so we headed to the hotel together and had a few minutes to get caught up with one another.

August 24th

I got up early, ready for a full day of media. I headed downstairs to the hotel lobby and met Cathy Cutz, a World

Vision media rep from Toronto who had been assigned to escort me throughout the day. What a nice girl.

We are moving the sponsorship drive into high gear today. My first interview was with Ron Able, the morning host at Winnipeg's country radio station, QX 104.1. Ron traveled to Honduras with us. It was great to see him again. We did an on-air interview, and then went to his office where he showed us his photographs from the mission.

Cathy surprised us both with news confirming our respective sponsorships of the Honduran children we had wanted to help. Marco and I had hoped to sponsor Genesis—Julio and Jennifer's daughter. I'm so glad that all of that is now in place and that the family will start to receive some relief.

Next I moved on to a TV interview with Sylvia Kuzyk, the weather anchor for CKY-TV. Sylvia had also been to Honduras. We shared a few tears and hugs as we recalled the trip and the powerful effect it had on us.

I continued the day with a few more radio and television interviews. In the evening, I did an outdoor acoustic performance for the public. This evening fundraising event was attended by the Mayor and a few other governmental officials as well as fellow artist Fred Penner. There were a lot of people there, and I'm so glad I could be a small part of it all. It's very powerful to witness people's generosity. Manitoba is proving to be very giving. Thank you.

August 25th

I was up early and flew to Sarnia, Ontario, today. We had a sold-out show tonight. We all love sellouts. They make my job so much easier and take the pressure off.

The show went great. A few of my family members were there, including my cousin Cindy from New Jersey and her four children. They just happened to be visiting the area. After the show, we all went back to my room to hang out and eat pizza. The family gathering included Aunt Barb and Uncle John; my cousin Debbie and her daughter, Amanda; Grandma

Verla and her friend Julie; my cousin Cindy and her kids, Anne, Code, Delaney, and Harper; as well as Eric Bartnes, my lighting director, and Lori Poremsky, my assistant. That's fourteen people in my room! It was cozy and fun.

August 26th

Up early again today. I flew from Sarnia to Toronto this morning. It's the day before my photo shoot for the Christmas album. At the insistence of Rob Waymen, the photographer, when I got to Toronto I had a spa day. It was so great. I had a pedicure, a manicure, a facial, and a full body massage. Whenever I take the time to do something like this, I'm surprised at how great it feels. It's something we should all do more often. For any of you men who may be reading this, I highly recommend a spa day for your girl. And for you girls who are reading this, it's a great gift suggestion. It took about four hours and the spa was right in my hotel, so after my treatments were finished, I returned to my room and ordered a nice light dinner. I'm feeling very relaxed and ready for a good night's sleep.

I hope the photo shoot goes well tomorrow. Photo shoots are always a bit challenging for me. They require more posing than I enjoy. I prefer to respond spontaneously. But it's something that has to be done and I'll hope for the best. I feel like there has been a good team assembled for the shoot, so we'll just see what happens.

August 27th

Well, from all that I can tell, the photo shoot went great! My good friend and makeup artist, Laura Szucs, was, in fact, able to be there. She takes such good care of me. She's also very funny; she helps bring a lightness to the proceedings. Laura and I have known each other for about ten years. We've seen each other go through a couple of boyfriends and some painful times. Now we celebrate each other's marriages. What a difference a few years can make. We've traveled

At the photo shoot for my Christmas CD. Laura Szucs fixes my hair, while Wendy deFreitas adjusts my wardrobe.
Photographer: Patrick Duffy

More primping at the photo shoot with Laura and Wendy.
Photographer: Patrick Duffy

Laura armed and dangerous with the leaf blower. Rob Waymen takes the shot, while Wendy looks on.
Photographer: Patrick Duffy

around North America together to a variety of award shows and events; we've had more than a few late-night conversations about love and life; and we've helped each other through some difficult times.

Once we did a two-day photo shoot in the Arizona desert. Those were long days. I was going through a break-up and it was very painful. I was so glad Laura was there. I would stay strong during the day, and she would help me do that. But once the photo shoot was done, I would go back to my room and cry my heart out, and she was there for me. (Thank goodness she was also good at covering up my puffy eyes.)

Fortunately, today's photo shoot had no sadness or life challenge attached, but like most photo shoots, we did encounter an obstacle or two. We needed a little bit of wind to blow my hair ever so slightly. The breeze from a fan was too strong; from a blow dryer, not strong enough. Laura, who does many fashion shoots, suggested we use a leaf blower. Well, we all thought that was a pretty outrageous suggestion, but Patrick Duffy, the art director and designer of the CD jacket, contacted his neighbor and borrowed his leaf blower. When he returned with the leaf blower, we all had some laughs: Rob would ask if we were all ready and there would be Laura, firing up this bulky leaf blower and trying to position it so the wind would be just enough to provide the desired effect on my hair. Of course we couldn't talk over the racket from the leaf blower, but we were all on the same page and very little communication was necessary. Moral: sometimes low-tech is high-tech.

Yes, it felt like a good photo shoot. Today's digital technology is amazing and useful. Almost as soon as a picture is taken, you can see the resulting image on a computer screen, enabling you to immediately adjust anything that may not be working, be it the set, the lighting, or the subject's hair, wardrobe, or makeup, for example. This immediacy speeds up the entire process, and increases everyone's confidence (especially mine) in the results. The stylist, Wendy deFreitas, was great. And I particularly enjoyed working with Rob Waymen—he's got an eagle eye.

I'm at my sister's house in Barrie as I'm writing this. The family came to pick me up after the shoot tonight, and I am going to spend the weekend here. I'm so glad to be here. I'm looking forward to helping around the house and just hanging out.

August 28th

I got a good sleep last night. As I opened my eyes this morning, there staring at me was my niece, Bryanna, saying enthusiastically, "Come on, Aunt Michelle, get up!" I always like to clean house for my sister, so she and Ed went off to work today and I cleaned house this morning, getting everything in order just in time for brother Steven to arrive.

Bryanna is at that age when she can help a little bit. She's so cute. We prepared a nice dinner for the family and we all spent the evening together. Oh, the simple things in life.

August 29th

We went to the hockey rink this morning to watch my nephew, Cody, try out for the hockey team. He's eleven years old and he's a goalie. It's great to see him all suited up and out there on the ice.

After the tryouts, we returned home and I decided that I wanted to share one of my childhood experiences with Bryanna. Watching *The Jungle Book* is one of my fond childhood memories. I particularly enjoyed the music. I wanted us to watch it together, so I went to the video store and rented it. We cozied up in the living room to watch. It was really fun, but to tell the truth, the cinematography is quite primitive compared to children's videos today. Bryanna enjoyed it, but I don't think she enjoyed it quite as much as I did at her age. It was a nice family day.

I fly home tomorrow and Marco comes home tomorrow night. I can't wait to see him.

August 30th

I flew home and went straight to the grocery store. I wanted to prepare Marco a nice, home-cooked meal. We're trying to eat well so we had scallops, baked red peppers, and steamed asparagus. Mmm...mmm.

August 31st

I did seven phone interviews between 8:45 a.m. and 11:30 a.m., and then I went into the studio to work on the final mixes for the Christmas record. We're getting there. We have just a few more over-dubs to do, the jingle bells as well as steel guitar and fiddle. I'm very pleased with how everything's sounding.

I hate to admit this, but Marco and I had a fight tonight— or a "disagreement" is more like it. He leaves for Texas tomorrow morning, so we won't really be able to talk this through. He needs to sleep tonight, so I'm actually quite proud of myself that I'm respecting the fact that he has a full day tomorrow and I don't need to keep him up hashing this out. I am not going to give details on our disagreement, and of course it's inevitable that we are going to have disagreements, but it still sucks.

September 1st

Marco left this morning, and I spent my time on the phone doing more interviews. We didn't get to talk a lot, which is probably just as well. The scary thing about being as independent as we are is that thoughts like "Well, I don't need this anyhow" certainly can crop up. I know it's not an uncommon thought in the heat of feeling misunderstood, but I hate it when that feeling rears its ugly head because the last thing I want is for my marriage to fall apart. You have to work through your stuff. Because this is Marco's and my first marriage I think I'm only now starting to realize that when you make the commitment in marriage, it is not something that you just casually walk away from. Marriage is for real, and as my manager says, "You either grow together or you grow apart."

I've been talking to Marco throughout the day. I'm really proud of how we have talked things through without tearing each other apart. That's what maturity will do for you. I think it's all still a soft spot, but I'm just going to not make a big deal out of this. I don't want to be a drama queen. I also recognize that we have both been traveling a lot and haven't had much time with each other. You really do have to make time for each other.

We did more mixes today in the studio. I'm tired. All this emotion is wearing me out. Oh, my life, so full of drama. Ha Ha Ha...Actually, now I'm looking forward to the making up part.

September 2nd

We left from Nashville early this evening for a show in Shawville, Quebec. We've got about a sixteen-hour drive ahead of us, so I'm sitting on the bus getting caught up on my journals. I love to hear the sound of the guys laughing and swapping stories and talking politics in the front lounge. That sounded so much like *The Waltons*. Don't let that fool you.

September 3ʳᵈ

The drive went fine last night and we arrived at about 10 a.m. this morning. There wasn't much to do today but journal.

Tonight's show started out great, but there was a beer tent located to the left of the stage. Since there was no drinking allowed outside of the beer tent, I watched as my crowd slowly divided into two groups. Those who wanted to have a cold beer and those who didn't. Once they got over to the beer tent, they could still see and hear the band, so many people did not return to their seats, opting instead to watch the band from over there. Oh well. Fortunately, it was a festival crowd of about eight thousand, so there was still a sizeable audience watching the show in front of the stage. I signed autographs, and we boarded the bus and headed on down the road.

September 4ᵗʰ

Sean and I performed this afternoon in Goderich, Ontario, at a grand opening for a new TSC store there. The bus dropped us off at a hotel in London at about 8 a.m. The rest of the gang carried on to Nashville, while we went back to sleep for a couple of hours. We were picked up at noon and driven to Goderich. Over twenty-two hundred people were there to meet us, the largest crowd we've ever had at one of these TSC events. Sean and I played some songs, and I signed autographs for several hours. It's always fun.

We drove back to Detroit to a hotel near the airport. We fly home tomorrow morning.

September 5ᵗʰ

Our flight home was uneventful, which, of course, is always good news.

I landed in time to catch the 11:30 a.m. church service. Today's sermon discussed finding your own truth about the

Lord and the Bible by asking questions and doing the research that you need. Becoming a Christian doesn't mean you are not going to have any questions about God, but you do have to find your own truth when it comes to your faith. You have to ask questions if you have them.

I think it's natural to have times of strong faith and times when it's not so strong. That's human nature and it's OK. When I hear other people of faith say that at times they struggle, it makes it real for me.

I picked up Gracie from the kennel. It's so much fun to see her, and I love how excited she always is to see me.

It's Mom's birthday today. We've been talking about her moving to Nashville. I would really like to have her here so we can spend more time together. It will be easier for Lori and the rest of the family, too, to travel here rather than to Tucson, Arizona. And Nashville's a strong real estate market, apparently one of the top ten in the country right now. Mom has been a real estate agent for at least twenty years. I think she would do well here, although starting over is never easy. Marco's being great about having his mother-in-law moving in for a couple of months, and I believe that Mom and Marco are going to become even better friends.

Our friends Mike and Tricia Basow, who got married a few months ago, are expecting a baby and have moved into a new house. I hadn't been there for the grand tour yet, so this afternoon I went over for a barbecue. It was nice to see them and their beautiful home.

September 6th

We finished the mixes for the Christmas CD today. I'm very pleased with the end results. I hope people will like what we've done.

I saw some of the pictures from the photo shoot and I'm happy to say that everything turned out great with the photography, too. Now we have to choose which pictures we want to use. We're very close to having a finished product.

Marco came home tonight. Considering that we haven't seen each other since our disagreement, it was so good to see him so we could just hug. Tomorrow we're going to spend the entire day together.

September 7th

A day off with Marco. Just what the doctor ordered.

September 8th

I cleaned house all day. We're having company tomorrow night, but I won't be here because I'm flying to Detroit again. Jack Bass, the supplier of Marco's Air Chairs, and his fiancée are coming to stay the night. They have some meetings to attend in Nashville. Jack is developing the new chair product Marco found for the business. He's bringing a prototype with him. I wish I could see it.

I feel like I've got everything ready for company. I'll pack tomorrow morning.

September 9th

I flew to Detroit tonight. A driver was there to pick me up and take me to a hotel in London, Ontario. We arrived around 9:15. I'm doing a photo shoot for TSC tomorrow. I'd better get some sleep.

September 10th

The photo shoot went great in London. Laura Szucs came down from Toronto to do my hair and makeup, and it was good to see her and work with her again.

We've got a show tomorrow night in Niagara Falls, Ontario, at a new casino called Casino Niagara. TSC arranged a limo for me this evening for the drive to the Falls. I love to play blackjack, so I couldn't resist playing a little when I arrived at the casino. As might be expected, I left a little bit of money behind, but I had fun. They say casinos aren't built on people's winnings.

This casino is a top-of-the-line entertainment complex. It feels like I'm in Las Vegas. The suite provided for the artists performing here is really beautiful and spacious. I have a fantastic view of the falls. They're lit up tonight just like they are every night, and it's so pretty.

September 11th

The Niagara Falls show went great. We had a wonderful time. The venue is so nice. Everything from the sound and lights to the stage itself is first-rate. The audience was also spe-

Photographer: Bill Borgwardt

cial tonight. Some nights are magic, and this was one of them.

I had some friends and family here for the show. Afterwards, we were being escorted back up to the suite via the typical behind-the-scenes route they use to move artists around the building. It was like a scene from *This is Spinal Tap*, particularly when we went through a dark hallway and our security guard couldn't get the door at the end to unlock. He was very apologetic. Fortunately, he had a two-way radio to summon help. I thought the situation was pretty funny, but he was quite concerned. Some of the artists he's worked with would have flipped out on him. I don't understand why someone would ever think people can be treated that way. Just because you sing for a living, just because you may be a "star," doesn't give you the right to be a jerk.

We finally got the door unlocked and made it to the suite. I had a chance to visit with the gang for a few minutes before it was time to board the bus and head home.

September 12th

I got home, went to church, picked up doggie, and had a nice day at home. Marco will be home tonight.

September 13th

Marco and I slept in and we had a nice day. We just hung out together.

I spent some phone time with Patrick and Brian reviewing the graphics for the Christmas CD booklet, making decisions about which pictures I want to be used. It's always a challenge to be objective about your own picture, but Brian is very helpful. I'm really pleased with this photo shoot, but it is still a challenge looking at oneself.

I also need to put together my thank yous for the CD. This is the easy part. I'm so thankful to all the people who helped me put this album together: the producers; the songwriters; the musicians; Robert, the photographer; Laura, my makeup artist; Wendy, the wardrobe stylist; Patrick, the art director; and Brian, for all his attention to detail. It takes a lot of work from a lot of people, and I'm excited about getting it out to the public. This year, the album is going to be available exclusively through TSC stores and at my shows. TSC is donating all the profits from the sale of the CD to World Vision Canada. I'm delighted.

Brian continues to organize our Christmas tour. It's coming together nicely. Like most of our projects, however, it requires a great deal of planning and thought.

I helped Marco load up the truck because he is leaving again tomorrow. It's so hard sometimes when he has to go, but I just can't put too much emotion into it because it is what it is—and it's not going to be for forever. Business is going well for both of us, so we'll just focus on the positive and give thanks.

September 14th

Marco left today. I'm going to do some housework and laundry and all that fun stuff.

September 15th and 16th

I spent a few hours each day working out and stretching, and taking advantage of this time to get myself in shape for our Christmas tour. It's going to be pretty demanding. I think we're starting around November 15th.

I'm leaving for a show in Calgary tomorrow, so I need to make sure all the regular things are taken care of. Gracie goes to the kennel, and Jeffery comes to feed the cats and cut the lawn.

September 17th

I got up early, had Gracie at the kennel by 7 a.m., and headed off to the airport. The trip to Calgary took all day. The flights were uneventful.

The show in Calgary is called "The Concert in the Meadows." It's a benefit for the farmers in western Canada struggling as a result of the mad cow disease scare. To simplify the logistics of the production, all the artists on this show will be working with the same band. I rehearsed with the band shortly after landing in Calgary. It was nice to see some of the same guys that I worked with when I did the Huron Carole Christmas tour last year.

Like the Huron Carole tour, the "Concert in the Meadows" is being organized by Tom Jackson. I can't really begin to quote all the figures, but millions of dollars have been lost because the farmers can't sell their cattle in America. I hope this benefit will help to bring awareness to the farmers' plight. Lisa Brokop is going to be performing as well as George Fox, Gil Grand, The Ennis Sisters, and Adam Gregory. Bachman-Turner Overdrive will be there for their last concert in Canada. The event should be fun, and it will be great to see all of the other artists.

I'm going to settle in for the night. I've got an early sound check.

September 18th

The show went well today. The band did a great job. I went out for dinner with Lisa and her brother/manager Dean. It was good to be able to spend some time hanging out. There is a party scheduled tonight for all the artists, but I'm calling it an early night because 5:30 a.m. comes pretty early.

September 19th

No matter how short of a time I've been gone, it's always nice to come home. I picked up Gracie; she always brings me joy. To all the dog owners out there, I know you know what I mean. I guess it's safe to say that our doggie is like our child. We're always so happy to see each other.

All in all, I had a pretty laid back day.

When I come home from the road, Gracie is always happy to see me.

September 20th

I had to deal with a lot of random stuff today. First I worked out. Then I had a conference call to make decisions about the Christmas album graphics. Then I started investigating the pros and cons of changing our family health insurance. Our current plan will not cover us if I get pregnant. We're not trying yet, but we are still talking about it.

Next I began the ordeal of getting all my personal documents legally changed. My documents are inconsistent. They bear a variety of names: either my birth name, my stepfather's name, or my married name. Because I travel to so many different countries, I need to simplify all of this and start carrying consistent documentation.

Needless to say, changing one's health coverage and having one's name legally changed require a ton of paperwork, too many phone conversations, and too much sitting on hold. Patience is a definite requirement, as is persistence.

September 21st

Songwriting, song listening.

September 22nd

Spent more time working on my name change and worked on the album graphics.

I got out all of our Hallowe'en decorations and put them up. The house looks great. This is Marco's favorite time of year, so I enjoy making it look like fall around the house.

September 23rd

I watched today's speech given by the Iraqi interim prime minister. I was so glad to hear him thank those who have helped free his people. But I'm so surprised by the insurgency—those members of the old regime who don't want freedom for their own people and continue to kill them. But I guess they were killing, enslaving, and controlling them before.

Obviously, I was raised to have a very different point of view about such things. It's a difficult thing to understand. I am absolutely concerned, wrapped up in the fact that America is at war. I pray everything will be all right.

September 24th

Today I watched a special on the country music sensation Big & Rich. They sure seem to be having a good time. I always celebrate fellow artists' success, especially when it happens for people who buck the system and do it their own way. I can never fathom why the powers that be in our industry so often seem to want more of the same. Why would you want another Keith Urban? We already have one. How about we try to find something different so that we can tell who's who? I don't profess to understand the record business, but I do get annoyed when you can tell that a project has been released hoping to capitalize on a trend.

I've enjoyed watching the rebellion of the Musik Mafia that's been underway here in Nashville and has spawned Big & Rich and Gretchen Wilson. Like it or not, their music has some passion and fire about it. I'm not suggesting that it's totally original. None of us are. But it is refreshing, because it sounds different from anything else currently going on.

September 25th

War and election. I'm not sure why it is that I've become so involved with the election this year because I can't vote in America. I guess for me, like for many people, 9/11 changed everything. The rose-colored glasses came off, and now I'm concerned about North America and our future.

It was the day after the 2001 Canadian Country Music Awards when 9/11 happened. Many artists were in Calgary for the awards show. None of us could get home because all flights were canceled.

That morning, Brian and I were about to head down to the hotel lobby to catch our ride to the airport, so I called him to see if he was ready. I had the TV on. It was while I was talking to Brian that I saw the second plane hit the World Trade Center. I remember saying to him I didn't think we were going to be going anywhere. I was right. It was four days later before we could get a flight home.

I was very depressed, feeling broken-hearted for the victims and their families. I think that, deep in my heart, I knew I was changed forever. I could never have imagined anything like that happening. I could never have imagined that type of evil. And now I knew it existed. I knew that nothing was ever going to be the same again. My naiveté was gone forever.

For the first couple of days, I did little more than stay in my room and sleep, all the while feeling a deep sadness.

I know that there is very little that I can do and that worrying is not the answer, so I don't worry much, but I do have a need to be more informed—to try to understand where these people are coming from. I also think it is really important to try and keep the terrorists at bay, if possible. They haven't attacked America since 9/11, so it appears that someone is doing something right. It all seems so confusing, and now that we're in the midst of an election campaign, everyone wants to lay blame, everyone's suggesting different or "better" ways of dealing with our challenges. Like so many of us, I simply don't have enough information to know what's really going on, and since all parties have their own spin, I'm not sure who or what to believe.

September 26th

Mom has decided to move to Nashville from Arizona and I feel really good about it. I want to have her close by, and this brings her closer to the rest of the family in Ontario, too. It's only a ten-hour drive or a short flight from Toronto. Maybe Lori and Ed will come and visit more often, although it's hard for them to get away because of their new business.

We have made the final decisions about the album graphics. It's nice to have that done. Now we can move on to the next items that need our attention. The most important item on my list is getting my country album finished.

Marco is coming home tonight. I'm going to Texas with him this week. I look forward to working with him and just being together.

September 27th

I wrote today with a girl named Maia Sharp. She's a wonderful talent. I've already recorded two of her songs for my next country project, "Something Wild" and "You Can't Lose Them All." Maia is also a recording artist. She enjoys a level of success on pop radio. I really like her voice as well as her writing.

I met her almost a dozen years ago at her home in California. She would have been about twenty at the time. I was there writing with her father, Randy, who had had a variety of cuts with a number of country artists, including Restless Heart. She has proven to be a great songwriter as well. Maia and her dad recently wrote the title track "Home" for the Dixie Chicks's current album. I also worked with her uncle, Steve, during my years at Arista Records. Steve did radio promotion, so we spent a lot of time together.

I found out about Maia through Brad, my sound engineer/road manager. He came across "You Can't Lose Them All" and brought it to me. Then I found "Something Wild" and heard a few of her other songs that I really liked. I knew I needed to follow up because it is rare for me to respond so strongly to a writer's work. It's important that I pay attention when that happens.

I really enjoyed writing with Maia, and I think we've started a good idea.

For the most part, however, I haven't been writing much recently. It's a really hard thing to do because I am looking for excellence, and nothing less. Tony Hazeldon's perspective is helpful here: for those of us who are trying to write something that has a different twist, it's just going to take more time, patience, and thought.

September 28th

Maia and I finished our song today. It's called "That's No Way To Live." I like it.

For many people, love seems to be a very scary thing. Many of us have been hurt in our relationships. We're disillusioned by love. So we live our lives afraid of heartbreak, afraid to open up our hearts to love. But living without love is no way to live:

> I've been afraid of love,
> Tossing and turning over what it is I'm so scared of.
> As soon as it begins I start wondering
> How it's going to end,
> And that's no way to live.

These are the kinds of things we talk about when I'm songwriting. Love and life and the challenge of figuring it out. There is no doubt some people have an easier time with all of this and some people struggle for many years. I once heard someone say that the life you build for yourself is the life you feel you deserve. Someone also told me that helping your children build high self-esteem is the best gift you can give them because from that they will make better choices for themselves.

September 29th

We were supposed to leave this morning for Texas, but we didn't get on the road until 7 p.m. Marco's truck was in the shop and it wasn't ready until then. We drove for six hours and found a hotel room. We'll finish the trip in the morning.

Mom arrived in Nashville this evening. We must have passed each other on the highway going in opposite directions. I wish we could have been there when she arrived, but things worked out differently. I left it up to her to decide when she wanted to come. All is well and I'm glad she's there safe and sound.

September 30th–October 3rd

Texas went really well for us. It's always good for me to go out and work a few days with Marco because we work our butts off and it feels good! This particular home show is in Canton, Texas, and, unlike many of the other shows he does, this one is held in the great outdoors. We can camp on the show grounds, and we do. We set up our tent and our booth and we're ready to go. I love that we're working in the outdoors and camping too.

Now let me caution you that this scene is not for anyone who is, or aspires to be, a diva. One has to enjoy camping and everything it entails to get the most out of this experience. Mind you, we do have a ten-by-twenty-foot tent with a seven-foot ceiling. And I do set it up like a little hotel room, with a king size air mattress and down pillows and blankets, nightstands with lamps, a refrigerator and a microwave, table and chairs, carpet, and, of course, a television. Often passersby will stop to peer into our tent and comment on how nice it looks. So maybe there is a little diva action going on, but it's important to me that I have a nice, cozy space when we camp out. But what means the most to me, of course, is that I'm with my Marco.

I love to watch Marco work because he's a super salesman. He brings a lot of energy to his work, and a great sense of humor. Grumpy Gus comes in and before you know it, Marco's got him sitting in an Air Chair, trying it out, and signing his Visa bill ready to leave, another satisfied customer. Marco has this ability to stay focused when he's chatting up a prospect, and he can stay on top of his game throughout the whole day. We often bring Gracie with us to Canton, and she thinks Marco's pretty good too.

We started tearing everything down around 4 p.m. Then, as tradition would have it, we went to Jerry's Pizza and got a pizza to go (actually with Marco, it's two pizzas) and, as usual, it was so good, and down the road we went, enjoying every bit of it. We decided to drive the ten hours straight through so we could get home to Mom. Marco drove while I rested, and then I took my shift. That made for a long day, considering we started in Texas at about 8 a.m. on Sunday and got home to Nashville at about 5 a.m. the following morning.

October 4th and 5th

Mom's here and we're getting her settled in. It's going pretty well. She has a nice bedroom upstairs, and a full living room and office area. She has her own private bath as well. Mom injured her knee skiing some years ago, however, so she is a bit concerned about climbing up and down the stairs. Hopefully we can sort that out.

Marco leaves for Indiana tomorrow. It's a quick turn-around since we just got home from Texas. I did what I could to help him, restocking his van with a new supply of Air Chairs for the next show. He usually does most of that work himself, but this time I wanted to help.

Marco will be gone for ten days to an event called the Parke County Covered Bridge Festival in Rockville, Indiana. Parke County is a historic area boasting thirty-two covered bridges. This is one of Marco's favorite shows. His hotel is about a half an hour away from the festival site. His drive to work takes him through some beautiful farmland, and now the leaves are starting to change color. Fall is Marco's favorite time of year, and he enjoys the ride twice every day. I've done this show with him before and it's really quite a scenic drive.

October 6th

Marco left this morning. I took care of some business, and then continued to get Mom settled in. We set up her office, and successfully added her computer to our wireless home system. I'm happy to announce I figured that out by myself. Computers are not my area of expertise. Surprisingly enough, when I hooked everything up and turned it on, it worked!

Mom's feeling a bit overwhelmed by all the reorganization, but I'm in my element. I enjoy the sense of accomplishment I feel when everything is in its place.

Mom has a Siamese cat named Coco. She is twenty years old and is not adjusting to the move as quickly as we had hoped. She's not too crazy about the fact that my entire animal family—especially Gracie—wants to welcome her to Tennessee. Gracie is used to the cats being her playmates. Coco, however, is not very happy about this and I'm not going to force the issue. I just hope she'll come out from under the bed someday.

October 7th

I sang in the studio all day today, recording my lead vocals for the country CD. I mostly worked on a song that I really love called "I Don't Want To Be That Strong," which was co-written by my producer, Tony Hazeldon, and Nashville singer/songwriter Tim Mensy. It's a relatable song about strength and vulnerability, the ironic story of a strong woman facing the prospect of a broken relationship. She knows she's strong enough to recover from heartbreak, but she doesn't want to rely on that inner strength:

Almost nothing shakes me
But I'll admit tonight I'm scared
Scared to death
All this talk of leaving
Walking away from love we've shared
Takes my breath
I could find the strength within myself

But I don't want to be that strong
I don't want to know that feeling
Of barely hanging on
While my broken heart is healing
I know the hands of time
Would hold me until all the hurt is gone
I know I could make it on my own
But I don't want to be that strong

So many women I know these days are strong and self-reliant. When life deals them a bad hand they figure it out, whether it means sacrificing to keep their family together or taking care of their children on their own. I also know many women like myself who are in charge; showing weakness is not easy for us. This song shows a vulnerability that I've learned to recognize in myself and even to admit. "Almost nothing shakes me / But I'll admit tonight I'm scared / Scared to death."

I feel like I have to do more work on my vocal performance because I want it to be great.

After singing, I came home and worked out. I don't seem to be losing any weight, but at least I'm not gaining any. I know I could be working harder, being more disciplined. That's one of my biggest challenges. I used to work out about two hours a day. Now I'm down to about four hours a week. I guess that explains it.

October 8th

I sang all day again and finished the vocal for "I Don't Want To Be That Strong." I'm very happy with it.

Mom and I went out for dinner to Omikoshi and took in a movie. We saw *Shark Tale*. It was a fine kettle of fish! I'm such a kid at heart; I really enjoyed it. Mom hadn't been to a movie for a while, so it was a lot a fun for her, too.

October 9th

I continued to settle Mom in. We did lots of sorting through boxes, some laundry, and had a fun day together getting things organized.

October 10th

Mom and I went to church today and then to lunch with all the gang that we met there.

After lunch, we went to some open houses so that Mom could start getting some sense of the domestic real estate market in Nashville. I love checking out the different homes. It doesn't matter whether they're newly built or fifty years old. I like looking at all the various design ideas and decorating schemes, so I enjoyed sharing that with Mom.

Next we rented a couple of movies. *Godsend* starring Robert De Niro, was pretty good, but we didn't like *The Ladykillers*, with Tom Hanks, at all. We got about twenty minutes into it and found all the profanity to be simply unnecessary. (Oh no, I'm starting to sound like my parents!) I'm not opposed to characters cursing in a movie, but this was over-the-top. Click!

October 11th

I seem to have strained my knee by carrying too much up and down the stairs. Talk about ironic: I didn't want Mom to worry about her knees, so I overcompensated.

While growing up, I was very active in sports. In grade eleven, I made it to the All Ontario Track and Field

Championships in the long jump. I jumped five meters, thirteen centimeters to qualify. I was so happy. Getting to this track meet was a big deal. But on my first jump there, I landed in the pit and my right knee went the wrong way. I was finished for the meet: my right leg was my kick-off leg from the board. I was really disappointed, but that's just the way it goes sometimes.

It appears I'm paying the price for that injury these many years later. I'll have to take it easy for a couple of days because I've got concerts coming up. We've got all the work around the house pretty much done, so I should be able to rest a bit.

October 12ᵗʰ

I wrote with Sarah Majors today. As always, it was great to spend some time with her. I'm not sure if we started a good idea or not. The stakes are high right now because we are trying to top the songs we already have. We'll have to get together and work some more on the idea.

I plan to record a song that Sarah wrote by herself called "Will You Love Me Anyway?" It's about a woman who, after putting her career ahead of having children, now wants to start a family, but has to face the issues of age and infertility in the context of her marriage. A number of women I know are dealing with similar situations. The song resonates for me because I too am confronted with the decision to have children or not—and my clock is ticking.

My knee is seriously hurt. I'm concerned about it. Patricia Conroy told me that something similar happened to her a while back. She's going to bring me the knee brace she used. You never realize how important your mobility is until you start to lose it. I'm not enjoying this at all. I'm used to going like ninety all day and I've been abruptly halted. I may have to get off my leg entirely and stay in bed. We'll see how I'm feeling tomorrow.

Patricia Conroy and her longtime love, Bob Funk, are finally getting married. I've always told her that when they did get married, I'd like to host the wedding at my house. Mom and I had lunch with Patricia and Billie Joyce today at Sunset Grill to start making plans for the wedding. October 21 is the big day. I'm really happy for her. They love each other and have been together for sixteen years, but Patricia wanted it to be official.

I got a scary phone call from Marco tonight. At first it didn't even sound like him. He was calling from a hospital to tell me he'd been in a head-on collision. I could tell by the tone of his voice that he was in shock or traumatized to some degree. But he assured me he was all right. He said he saw the car coming at him and there was nothing he could do; it happened so fast.

Thank God Marco's all right. He had a CAT scan because his head hit the windshield on impact. He doesn't wear his seat belt. Maybe now he will.

He was enjoying his usual evening drive back to the hotel room when a guy in a Saturn came barreling around a corner. Marco could tell that he was going too fast. Before he knew it, the car hit him head-on. Needless to say, it was a pretty traumatic experience. Both vehicles were totaled, but no one was seriously hurt.

I think I'm in a bit of shock myself right now because I could have lost him. I guess that's how quickly it happens. Fortunately, those farm roads twist and turn a lot and you can only go so fast. I'm feeling helpless because Marco's in Indiana and I'm here in Nashville. He's handling it very well, and that's keeping me from worrying. We'll talk tomorrow about his plans. He said he's going to get some rest tonight, rent a car to get to work tomorrow, and deal with things as he can. I guess I better get some sleep as well.

October 14th

Patricia, Billie Joyce, and Colette Wise came over and we continued to make plans for Patricia's wedding. I'm going to decorate the house and ready the yard, and all the girls are going to prepare food. We are going to make it a potluck like we've done so many times before. There is always plenty to eat and drink. Lori Kerr is going to make the cake. The same pastor that married Marco and me is going to preside over the wedding. What a celebration it will be!

I'm concerned about my knee. Patricia brought over her knee brace and I'm going to spend the rest of the night in bed.

October 15th

Well, my knee is not getting any better. Today I stayed in bed and rested. Of course there's never a convenient time for this. I need to get ready for the road, but the best thing I can do right now is rest.

October 16th

I stayed in bed half the day and then packed and got ready to head out of town. The knee brace works very well. It seems to give support. I'm going to wear it as much as I can. We boarded the bus at midnight for London, Ontario. We are doing a full band show there for TSC Stores. This show is a bit different for us because we are also actively participating in the company's annual Managers' Conference. Tomorrow I will attend one of their meetings to talk about how and why I came to be TSC's corporate spokesperson, and how I'm feeling about my association with the company. (I'm really enjoying it.) At that meeting, I'm also going to deliver the finished Christmas album to TSC. John Kropp and I will talk about how TSC and I have joined forces to produce *A Wright Christmas* exclusively for their stores this holiday season. And I'll get to mention how thrilled I am that all profits from TSC's sale of the CD will be donated to World Vision Canada.

That's incredible!

After the meeting, it will be dinnertime. All the TSC folks and the band and I are going out to a sports bar to have supper and participate in some kind of mysterious team-building exercise. It's been rumored to involve some games, such as pool and bowling. I love games. It should be fun.

October 17ᵗʰ

We arrived in London at 1:15 p.m. I settled into my room and got ready for the meeting. There were about fifty managers and other TSC executives there, and it was nice to see everyone. I have met many of these people at a store opening or two. I shared with everyone how I felt about my relationship with TSC and that I was looking forward to our continued association. Next we presented the Christmas CD. It is a

My Christmas CD (booklet front cover).
Photographer: Rob Waymen. CD Booklet Art Direction and Design: Patrick Duffy

beautiful package and I'm very proud of it.

After the meeting and a short break to get ready for the evening, everyone gathered in the hotel lobby where each of us were assigned to one of three teams: orange, green, or turquoise. We donned our team T-shirts, boarded a school bus, and headed out to this cool game facility. Each team assembled at its first designated game area and the competition began. There was bowling, pool, basketball, and car racing challenges for each team, followed by delicious pizza. It was a lot of fun. I hate to admit it, but my team, Team Orange, came in last. (All my years of hanging out at pool halls and bowling alleys gave me no unfair advantage whatsoever.) Apparently, my band members acquitted themselves well; Brian, however, shared my misfortune as a fellow member of Team Orange. Thankfully, my knee held up okay.

Our show is slated for tomorrow night's banquet after all the awards are handed out to TSC's top achievers for the year.

October 18th

The show went well. It was an intimate gathering. Most of these people have seen our full blown show, so we scaled things back a bit and kept it more personal. We loaded the bus and headed home. Marco is home now and I haven't seen him since the accident so I can't wait to give him a big hug.

October 19th and 20th

Patricia's wedding is only a few days away. I had a lot to do today. She let me know how she would like the decorations to look. She wants white flowers and white lights. Right now my house is all decorated in fall colors, but I am more than happy to take down the Halloween decorations and replace them with her desired decor. I have the idea in my mind and I'm looking forward to getting it all done when we can finally light the candles and plug in the lights inside and out.

Mom and I did yardwork. We trimmed all the bushes and put up the lights. Here in Nashville, the weather is still warm enough to have an outside party, so this will be an indoor/outdoor party. It's nice to have Mom here because she's so helpful. I may have felt a bit overwhelmed myself without her help.

As long as I keep the brace on my knee, it seems to feel better. I hope this is going to heal without any further medical attention.

October 21st

Today was the big day. We got everything done in time for the guests to start arriving. Patricia, of course, looked beautiful. And, for the first time, we all saw Bob in a suit. He looked so handsome! I think all the decorations looked spectacular. Everything went off without a hitch. The food was delicious and the weather was perfect. I asked Marco if he would mind picking up a couple of bouquets of white flowers: in typical Marco style, he came home with about twelve bou-

My Ya-Ya Sisterhood at Patricia and Bob's wedding. Front row: Shelly Kerwin, Tia McGrath, Laurie Kerr, and Arlene Gold. Back row: Yours truly, Diane Morrison, Dinah Brien, Allison Taylor, Patricia Conroy, Colette Wise, Laurie Soules, Laurie Hildebrandt, Billie Joyce, Loretta Brank, and Carolyn Dawn Johnson.
Photographer: Lee Ann Burgess

quets. It looked so beautiful having fresh white flowers around the house.

Carolyn Dawn Johnson also attended. She is a busy young lady these days, but she makes time for her friends and that's just another thing that makes her so special.

It's really nice to have that many friends together at one time. It seems that with our busy lives and traveling we don't get enough time to hang out.

We danced and we celebrated and the party lasted into the wee hours. A fine time was had by all. Everyone kicked in to help clean up. When it was all said and done you almost wouldn't have known that we had just had a party for about forty people. Gatherings like this, I think, help us all recognize how lucky we are to have great friends and family.

October 22nd

Marco was up early and off to work. I don't know how he does it. I swear he has more energy than I do. I cleaned house and put up all the Hallowe'en decorations once again. We're back to normal. I'm glad there are leftovers from last night because I'm tired and I don't feel like cooking.

October 23rd

Marco wants to get a big cube van and find a warehouse for all his stock. He'd been thinking about the cube van even before the accident. Now, since his own van is totaled and he no longer has a vehicle to drive for work, the idea has become a top priority. He's been renting a cube van until he finds one he'd like to buy. Mom's been looking, and I think she may have found a couple. We need to get out there and look around some more. Also, we have to find warehouse space. Marco's business is growing and he needs more room.

I'm going to do a very thorough job of cleaning up the garage today and organizing all of the Air Chair stock. It will be nice when we get a warehouse because then I'll have the garage back. It's served its purpose for Marco's business, but he's outgrown it.

My knee is feeling better.

October 24th

Marco went to work this morning. Mom and I attended church, had lunch with the gang, and then we went to the flea market. On our way back to the car, we saw a line of cube vans waiting to load the merchants out. I stopped and asked a guy about his truck. He happened to mention that his brother worked at a bank and they had just repossessed a truck like his. He said it was in great shape, with only a few thousand miles on it. It sounds exactly like what Marco is looking for. He's going to check it out tomorrow.

Mom and I went to a movie tonight with a group of friends. We saw *Shall We Dance?* with Richard Gere, Susan Sarandon, and Jennifer Lopez. It was a nice, romantic movie.

October 25th

I had a meeting with Tony, Russ, and Brian to discuss the remaining recording. After the meeting, we listened to some more songs, but we didn't hear anything. Then I did some more singing. It was a tough day because I'm pretty hard on myself. I know how I want the songs to sound, and until they do, I will not be satisfied.

In November, I have another grand opening scheduled for a TSC store in Walkerton, Ontario. Sean, my guitarist, isn't available, so I asked Marco if he wanted to do the show with me. I didn't expect him to say yes, but he did. I'm so happy he accepted the opportunity for him and me to play a gig together. It should be fun.

October 26th

My knee is better. The body's ability to heal is an amazing thing. I was getting concerned because I thought I may have to have surgery or go for physical therapy, and I have a lot of work and touring to do, so there's no time for that.

I sang in the studio all day. It's coming together.

October 27th

Marco left for Texas.

Mom left for Arizona. She's going back to Tucson to finalize the sale of her home and to try and sell a house for another client while she's there. I hope the visit will allow her to finally settle in her heart whether the move to Nashville is good for her. I hope she feels good about her decision because it's nice to have her here.

After Tucson, I think Mom may travel to Barrie to help out there for a week or so. Lori and Ed are moving their business to a new building and are planning a grand opening, so Mom wants to be there to help out.

I sang all day. When I say "all day," it usually means from about 10 a.m. until 5 p.m., with a short break for lunch. That's about all the time my attention deficit will allow me before we start getting diminishing returns. I'm feeling pretty good about everything.

October 28th

I sang all day again, and as I was leaving the studio, Rhoda Kershaw, a friend of Russ and Debbie's, stopped by. I have met Rhoda a few times and thought she was a really special lady. Well, today I was surprised to learn she is a survivor of the international sex slave trade. She told me about a fundraising dinner being held in Nashville this evening for the International Justice Mission (IJM), an organization based in Washington, DC, which rescues victims of violence, sexual exploitation, slavery, and oppression around the world, and asked me if I would like to attend. Debbie and Russ were going. I said I would too.

At the fundraiser, we heard Gary Haugen, the founder of IJM, describe the work of the organization through the stories of victims that were helped. I'm glad I went because of the awareness I gained, but it breaks my heart to learn that people treat each other this way. How do people sleep at night knowing they make their living as sex traffickers? How can they abuse children so? It is unimaginable to me.

Martina McBride was the honorary chairperson of this evening's event, which brought the music industry together to show support for International Justice Mission's fight against oppression. After dinner, I was able to introduce Rhoda to Martina. The event raised more than one hundred thousand dollars to help IJM with its good work.

October 29th

It was a full day. I did some voice-overs for some TSC radio commercials and worked some more on the *Women of Country* demo.

I also scheduled rehearsals for the Christmas Tour. Everyone in the band and crew is available on the days I think will work best. We're all looking forward to the tour. I hope it goes as well as last year. We're calling it the I'm Dreaming of a Wright Christmas Tour 2004. We've doubled the number of shows we're doing this year. It will be good to tour with the Christmas CD available.

October 30th

I cleaned house and then went to a Hallowe'en party at Bob and Patricia's. She showed us her wedding gifts. We had a chance just to hang out without the pressure of it being her wedding day.

We watched Carolyn Dawn Johnson on the *Grand Ole Opry*. She looked and sounded great. Then the next thing we knew, she was knocking at the door and joining us at the party!

Some people came dressed up. I came as Michelle Wright. We had fun.

Three fine young Canadians. Visiting with my friends Carolyn Dawn Johnson and Patricia Conroy.

October 31st

I went to church and once again had a great lunch with my friends.

Tonight was Hallowe'en. I live in a great neighborhood full of kids. It was a warm night, so we had a lot of trick-or-treaters.

Jimmy Olander and his wife Claudia came by with their kids, Max and Eli. They are fostering Eli right now and hoping they can adopt him. They adopted Max a couple of years ago. It has been great to see him grow. He is so cute.

This is the first time that I have been this connected to adoption. I have enjoyed watching Jimmy and Claudia become a family with their kids. They are very happy with their decision to adopt and would recommend it to anyone. Who knows, it may be something Marco and I end up doing.

November 1st

Tony and I spent the morning listening to songs in various publishers' offices on Music Row. I'm not sure if we heard anything we'd want to record. We heard some really good material, but now that we're down to the last couple of songs, the stakes are high. Really good isn't good enough.

After lunch, I went to the studio and sang for the rest of

the afternoon.

November 2nd

I sang all day and then went to the gym. My knee is really bothering me. I'm not sure going to the gym was the best decision. I wonder what I'm going to do about this. As long as I don't do very much, my knee is fine. But I lead a very active life and that won't work. I keep hoping the knee's just going to heal itself. I may have to go to the doctor.

November 3rd

I sang all day. Recording my lead vocals requires a lot of focus and discipline. Typically, I'll start my day in the studio by singing the particular song on which we're working three or four times from beginning to end. Then Russ, Tony, and I will listen to all of these performances to determine what we like about them, and what, if anything, needs to be improved.

When I was first making records, I would leave a lot of the critical listening and the resulting decisions solely to my producers. These days, however, I prefer to be deeply involved in the whole process of developing the lead vocals. Russ and Tony welcome my input.

Once we've fixed anything that was bothering us, once we're certain we've captured the emotion appropriate for the material, we'll start to experiment. I may play with the phrasing of the lyrics or alter the melody somewhat, all with the object of enhancing the song's emotional impact. Some days the whole process goes very smoothly and you feel like you're really nailing what the song needs. Other days the process is more challenging. Some songs require more effort.

At the end of the day the guys will burn a CD for me and I'll take it home and listen to it that evening. If I like what we've done, we'll move on to another song the next day. If not, it's back to the drawing board.

November 4th

Another day in the studio singing. I'm feeling pretty good about how my vocals are turning out, and I'm enjoying working with Russ and Tony. These two guys are very different, yet they're fast friends. Russ hails from Indiana via Texas and the famed Muscle Shoals, Alabama, recording scene. He's been a drummer, so he understands music thoroughly. As a recording engineer, he handles most of the technical stuff. Russ has also been a music publisher for many years. He has found many hit songs for artists, including "Achy Breaky Heart" for Billy Ray Cyrus and "Take It Like A Man" for me. There's no question Russ knows a great song when he hears one. He brings a tremendous intensity and energy to the recording process, and I'm glad he's a part of the team.

Tony, on the other hand, is a laid-back Louisianian. He was born in South Carolina, but raised in bayou country. Tony is a brilliant guitarist, a wonderful singer, and an award-winning songwriter with #1 hits to his credit such as George Strait's "You Know Me Better Than That" and Colin Raye's "That's My Story." He's also one of the founding members of LeRoux, a seminal Southern rock band founded in Baton Rouge in the late seventies. Being a singer himself, Tony is particularly helpful as we develop my vocals: he always has suggestions for phrasing, rhythm, and melody. I find him to be a very calming influence in the studio (and sometimes I really need that).

Together, Russ and Tony have produced hit records for the Kinleys and the Wilkinsons, among others. We've been having fun doing these projects together.

November 5th

Another day in the studio singing.

On our meal break, I hooked up with Claudia Olander and some friends to go to a fundraising luncheon for the Miriam's Promise adoption agency. What a wonderful organization! Its mission is to find homes for children, and kids for couples who want to be parents. Learning about Miriam's Promise filled my heart with joy. I had a chance to meet some of the kids and their families.

Claudia and Jimmy are hoping they can adopt Eli through Miriam's Promise. It's up to the birth mother to make the decision based on the information that she has received about three potential sets of parents, including Jimmy and Claudia. The birth mother is apparently not allowed to know that Jimmy and Claudia have been fostering Eli. It's an emotional time for our friends. I sure hope they can adopt him because they are two of the finest people I know. They have so much love for Max and Eli.

I went back and sang for the rest of the day, and then Marco and I went to Pat and Celeste's for the evening. Celeste prepared a wonderful meal, including fresh bread with sliced tomatoes and basil dipped in an Italian-spiced balsamic vinaigrette, with a delicious grilled eggplant entrée. We stayed late, laughing and getting caught up with each other's lives. Lots of fun was had by all.

November 6th

I got up and went grocery shopping and spent the better half of the day preparing a variety of things. For fun I tried to do something a little different using a couple of new recipes. I prepared tuna with capers, and a sesame seed asparagus dish, but I'm not sure how successful the outcome was. It wasn't bad—it just wasn't great. A split decision from the jury.

Marco and I had a relaxing night together.

November 7th

We had another inspirational morning at church, lunch with our friends afterwards, and a quiet day around the house.

November 8th

I listened to some songs at home today. The challenge continues.

Marco and I have been rehearsing for the TSC store opening. It's going well. Marco is working hard and his guitar playing sounds great. However, I think his fingers might be getting a little sore. He hasn't played his guitar this much in quite a while.

I'm busy with preparations for the Christmas tour. Decisions have to be made about the songs we're going to play and how our stage is going to look. Lee Warren, my band leader, has circulated *A Wright Christmas* to all the band and crew.

November 9th

I had lunch with the band at Taste of India to discuss our plans for the Christmas tour. By now everyone has listened to the Christmas CD, so we were able to talk about the music and how we can present it. Everyone is looking forward to the tour. I appreciate my band members' input. I enjoy incorporating their ideas into the show (or at least considering them).

November 10th and 11th

I went wardrobe shopping for the Christmas tour. I have a few things in my closet that I can use, but I was hoping to find a few other pieces. I did find some jewelry and jeans.

I had my hair done today, bringing it back to my natural color. Marco really likes it. I'm in a bit of shock because I can't believe how dark it is.

Marco and I rehearsed some more today. The music is coming together well. I also did more preparation for the Christmas tour. My lighting director and stage designer, Eric "Cartman" Bartnes, and I are creating the set design. So far, we've decided on the following items:

> two six-foot high, 600-light Christmas trees;
> one light-up star prop;
> six long plastic icicles;
> five bags of fake snow; and
> one hockey bag full of miscellaneous red, white, and black fabric

We're also planning to include several of Eric's favorite stuffed animals: Timmy and his dog, Strobe; the penguins, Jesus and Christo; two owlets, Who and Who Else; Murray the sheep; and last, but not least, Bonhomme the stuffed snowman.

Never a dull moment when you're working with Cartman!

Someone has broken into our bank account. Apparently, the robbery is tied into some kind of scam going on in Romania, if you can believe that. We're not sure how they got access to our debit cards, but the bank has insurance for such things, so we will be getting all our money back. We had to cancel all our debit cards and I'll have to redo all of our bills that are paid automatically. It will take some time, but the good news is that all we'll lose is some time.

November 12th

Brian, Marco, and I left for the TSC store opening in Walkerton. We flew from Nashville via Detroit to London. TSC's John Couper picked us up at the airport and brought us to the store for an evening sound check.

Marco had never driven through this part of Ontario, but since Brian was born in the area, he was only too happy to serve as our tour guide. Marco and Brian both have a good sense of humor. When they get together, it can be pretty funny—lots of jokes, lots of "pun"ishment.

For example:
Brian: Hey Marco, we're driving through Perth County now. What do you think this area's famous for?
Marco: I dunno, bro. What?
Brian: Manufacturing handbags.
(Sigh. Of course, guys being guys, there has to be lots of one-upmanship:)
Marco: So what do the farmers grow around here?
Brian: I'm not sure. I think Michelle's family used to grow soybeans in Kent County, though.

Marco: Well, tomorrow, in honor of all the Ontario farmers, why don't we rename one of the carols we're playing and call it "Soy to the World"?

Help me. Somebody help me. My manager's a punner and I married another one.

We stopped for a bite en route to Walkerton and arrived at the new store at 9 p.m., right at closing time. The sound system brought in for tomorrow's event was already set up. With the store being closed, Marco and I could take as much time as we needed to run through our songs and get ready for the show.

We got to our hotel around 11 p.m. It's nice to have Marco here with me. I hope everything goes well tomorrow. We've practiced enough. We're ready.

November 13th

The show went great. Marco was great, though he told me afterwards that his fingers were killing him. We had a big crowd, about eighteen hundred people, and sold a couple hundred Christmas CDs, raising a good sum of money for World Vision.

We arrived at the store just after 8:30 a.m. While Marco was tuning our guitars and doing a little last-minute rehearsal, I spent about an hour in the back warehouse area "meeting and greeting" with the store staff, signing autographs, taking pictures, and visiting with some of the TSC employees who had come in from head office and other stores for the opening. At around 10 a.m., Roy Carter and John Kropp from TSC; Charlie Bagnato, the mayor of the Municipality of Brockton; Chad Denstedt, the TSC store manager; Dale Sewers, the assistant store manager; and yours truly headed out to a stage which had been put up in the middle of the store and the official grand opening ceremony began. After a few words from the TSC executives and the mayor, it was time for my part in the festivities.

Now at most grand openings, there's usually some sort of

ribbon-cutting ceremony. Not so at a TSC store opening. In keeping with their slogan, "the Incredible Country Hardware Store," TSC openings feature a chain-cutting ceremony! So while Roy Carter and the mayor held an eight-foot length of chain between them, John Kropp handed me a pair of heavy-duty chain cutters and I cut that chain in two.

Everyone else left the stage. I took the microphone and welcomed the crowd to the new Walkerton store. I explained I was there to sing a bit and sign some autographs. Then I introduced my accompanist, who had taken the stage while I was talking to the crowd. Marco was very concerned about being unobtrusive for this show: he absolutely did not want to be introduced as my hubby. (I don't think he wanted the added pressure of people staring at him while he was trying to

Chain-cutting ceremony at TSC store opening in Walkerton, Ontario. From left: Mayor Charlie Bagnato, moi, TSC's John Kropp, Chad Brockton, Dale Sewers, and Roy Carter.
Photographer: John Couper

get through the show.) We had discussed his reluctance to be introduced that way, and we had decided we could best handle things by giving him a stage name. Marco suggested we call him "Jimmy Paluso," who is a childhood schoolmate, so today I introduced him as "that famous guitar player from Nashville—Jimmy Paluso!" As the crowd roared their appreciation for this new member of the Michelle Wright team, we strapped on our guitars and got through the first three-song set without a hitch.

Marco left the stage once the set was finished and I moved to an area in front of the stage, where I sat at a table and started signing autographs. After about an hour of signing, I realized I needed to get some information from Brian, who was back in the store's office. Marco was up on stage again, tuning our guitar for the next set, so I turned to him and asked, "Hey, Billy! Can you go to the back, please, and tell Brian I need to see him for a moment?" Marco replied with a mischievous smile, "Yeah, sure...But it's *Jimmy*, not *Billy*." Well, at that, Marco and I started laughing, and the TSC folks in the vicinity (all of whom were aware of the stage name situation) started howling with laughter, too.

Just after 11:30 a.m., Marco and I performed our second set. Before the last song, I told the audience I had a surprise for them, and I shared our secret with everyone. The crowd was delighted to find out it was my hubby, Marco, up there on stage with me. "Jimmy Paluso" was quickly forgotten, and Marco's presence in Walkerton became quite the topic at the autograph table for the rest of the opening. For all of us, it seemed like a little extra magic dust had been sprinkled on the event.

We left Walkerton at around 1:30 p.m. and retraced our route to the London airport for a 4 p.m. departure for home. When we arrived in London, we had enough time for the obligatory visit to Harvey's. While we were standing at the counter waiting for our orders, Marco struck up a conversation with the waitress.

"So, do you like country music?" he asked in his best

Nashville accent. Getting an affirmative reply, he went on. "Who are some of your favorite artists?" She named a couple, and Marco continued, "Have you ever heard of Michelle Wright?"

"Yeah, of course," the waitress replied, warming up to the conversation. "In fact, she once babysat my younger brother."

Well, I couldn't resist. I stepped forward and blurted, "I did?"

The waitress heard my voice, looked over at me, made one of those "omigod" expressions, and covered her mouth with her hand. We talked some more. Apparently I had, indeed, babysat her younger brother way back when. I signed an autograph for her and turned around to get some ketchup and vinegar for my fries.

The waitress looked back at Marco. "Are you a country star, too?"

Marco smiled. "Have you ever heard of Jimmy Paluso?"

The poor dear thought for a moment. "Yeah...I think so."

Enough was enough. I grabbed "Jimmy" by the arm and we made a quick getaway.

Our flights home were uneventful. We made it safely to Nashville by 9 p.m. What a whirlwind trip.

November 14th

We went to church early this morning, the 8:30 a.m. service, and then had brunch with Joey and Bonnie. We haven't spent any time with them, so it was nice to get caught up. We talked about their plans for the wedding. Things are still a bit up in the air.

All afternoon and into the evening, I rehearsed with the band for the Christmas tour. Rick Marks, my drummer, drove in from his home in Lexington, Kentucky. We met at Brad's house. He's got a great space for rehearsing and we tend to use it a lot. The show we've organized has two fifty-minute sets, each featuring a mixture of material from *A Wright Christmas* punctuated, of course, by the hits. Things seem to be coming together pretty well.

November 15th

I did interviews for the Christmas tour and had another rehearsal with the band. I have to pack tonight because we leave to start the tour tomorrow. Rehearsal went well and I'm ready to go.

November 16th

We left for the Christmas tour today. I'm feeling pretty relaxed about everything, particularly compared to last year. I don't know if I've ever been as uptight as I was last year before our first Christmas show. It was just so different from anything I had ever done, and I was hoping the audience would like it. We had a fantastic time last year, and here we go again. This year our friend Lori Poremsky is coming out with us to be my personal assistant and to help out Lee, who doubles as our merchandiser as well as our band leader. We're picking

My band and me, all ready for our Christmas tour. From left: Dan Nadasdi, Lee Warren, Rick Marks, and Sean Smith.

Lori up in Detroit.

We got away a bit later then expected due to miscommunication with the bus company about our departure time. Then, a couple of hours down the road, the bus caught on fire. It seems to have something to do with its main air conditioner. We'll have to run the secondary air conditioner off the generator, and fix the other when we can. Hopefully, this start is not indicative of things to come. I also hope these delays are not going to put us too far behind for our first load in. (I'm not showing my concern to the band because that doesn't do any good.)

As with any tour, I have to adjust to the idea of being away from home for a longer period of time than I'm used to. But in a few days, I'm sure I'll have adjusted to my other life out here on the road.

November 17th

Brian called to tell me all of our shows are sold-out on our Northern Ontario run! Our first show tonight was in Cobalt, Ontario, at the Classic Theatre, a beautifully restored concert hall. The show went flawlessly, and the audience was really enthusiastic. After the show, I signed autographs in the lobby. It was so cool to have a Christmas CD available for the fans. The crew loaded up the gear, and we headed down the road for Geraldton. Everyone is feeling good, but we're all a little tired.

November 18th

The 420-mile trip to Geraldton went fine. We've got a great bus driver, Allan Funderburke, with us for this tour. He takes command of that driver's seat, and he rolls us along smoothly. It's imperative to travel with a top driver—someone experienced and responsible—especially considering the treacherous winter road conditions we're liable to encounter on this tour, particularly in Northern Ontario. We're hauling a large trailer behind the bus, filled with instruments, sound equipment, lights, and materials for our stage set. Trailers can be unwieldy. Whenever you're pulling one, the bus driver has to be even more careful.

We arrived in Geraldton in time for breakfast and ready for another day on the road. Here's a typical tour day schedule for the Michelle Wright organization:

8:00 a.m.   Local sound and lighting company arrives at venue and starts setting up their equipment.

10:00 a.m. Michelle Wright bus arrives at hotel. Michelle and most band members stay at hotel. Brad, Eric, Rick, and bus driver take bus to venue.

10:30 a.m. Bus driver returns to hotel. Brad meets briefly with tonight's concert promoter, checks in with local sound and light company to make sure everything is on schedule, and answers any questions about the day.

11:30 a.m. Local crew helps Brad unload our equipment out of the bus and trailer. Eric starts working with lighting crew to install and refine lighting installation.

12:00 p.m. Brad and Rick start setting up Rick's drums and the sound equipment we carry with us (sound console, microphones, and cables).

12:30 p.m. Deli tray and drinks for band and crew arrive in band's dressing room.

1:30 p.m.   Local runner drives band members from hotel to venue.

2:00 p.m.   Band members set up their guitars and keyboards.

2:30 p.m.   Sound check starts.

2:45 p.m.   Runner drives Michelle from hotel to venue.

3:00 p.m.   Michelle and band sound check, and rehearse if needed.

5:00 p.m.   Catered dinner at venue for Michelle, band, and crew. Brad turns in guest list for tonight to venue box office.

5:30 p.m.   Michelle (and anybody else that wants to go) returns to hotel to clean up and dress for show.

6:00 p.m.   Lori P. and World Vision rep set up their merchandise and display tables in venue lobby.

6:45 p.m.   Brad and Eric check to make sure stage is clean, and water and set lists are in place.

7:00 p.m.   Venue doors open.

7:15 p.m.   Band returns from hotel.

7:30 p.m.   Michelle returns from hotel.

7:50 p.m.   Everyone puts on their headset microphones and ear monitors and assembles backstage.

8:00 p.m.   Emcee introduces Michelle and show starts.

8:50 p.m.   Intermission.

9:10 p.m.   Second set starts.

10:00 p.m. Show ends.

10:10 p.m. Brad brings Michelle to autograph table. Brad, Eric, band, and local crew start tearing equipment down.

11:00 p.m. Brad and local crew load out stage gear to the bus.

11:30 p.m. Runner brings bus driver from hotel to bus. Michelle finishes signing autographs. Lori or Lee brings Michelle to bus. Lori and World Vision rep strike their tables.

12:00 a.m. Bus departs for the next city.

For this tour, we're working closely with World Vision Canada to raise awareness of their child sponsorship program. Hopefully, some people who attend our shows will become

On the road with my band, crew, and bus. From left: lighting director Eric Bartnes, guitarist Sean Smith, tour manager/front-of-house sound operator Brad Burkett, bus driver Allan Funderbunke, drummer Rick Marks, keyboardist Dan Nadasdi, and guitarist Lee Warren.

sponsors just like Marco and me. World Vision has sent a representative out on the road with us to operate a table in the lobby where audience members can choose to sponsor a child if they wish. His name is Michael Kelly. Tonight was Michael's first night with us, and I think he is going to fit in just fine. We had another great show this evening, and five kids got sponsored.

We'll be staying here tonight and driving on to Terrace Bay tomorrow morning.

November 19th

November 19th

Tonight, the show in Terrace Bay felt very special. Six kids were sponsored. A couple of people with special needs presented me with a lovely bouquet of flowers. I asked them to stay and sing with me. It was one of those magical moments on stage that you can't plan. There wasn't a dry eye in the house.

Mom will be visiting for a while longer with Ed and Lori. They still need her help.

Marco is enjoying his days off before the Christmas onslaught begins. He sets up booths in a couple of malls around town. He may actually do more than two malls this year. It's a twelve-hour-a-day job in each mall, so he is hoping to put a couple of guys to work. He's considering hiring two full-time salespeople and adding more Air Chair shows to the schedule.

We're staying here in Terrace Bay tonight.

November 20th

We played Manitouwadge tonight and got four kids sponsored. Once again it was another great show.

We had a funny incident tonight. During our first set, my lighting director noticed that a significant number of his lights weren't working. Eric couldn't leave his lighting board to figure out what was going on, however, until intermission. At the break, he went backstage and discovered the problem.

Someone had wanted to make a cup of coffee. Unfortunately, when he plugged in the coffee pot, he unplugged a third of our light show! That's funny. Eric behaved very well. Instead of smashing the coffee pot, he calmly unplugged it and plugged his lights back in. At least that's what he told me he did.

Brian called first thing this morning to say he had received a very complimentary e-mail about the show from the promoter in Terrace Bay. He e-mailed it to me, and here's what she wrote:

Dear Brian,

It's after 3 a.m. and I'm still so high up from tonight's concert that I just may not sleep at all. I just wanted to say that Michelle Wright and company truly epitomizes the word "entertainment." While very professional from start to finish, there was a very relaxed atmosphere from the get-go. We were able to accommodate an earlier stage call than negotiated (1 p.m.—but they arrived at 12:15 p.m.—yet it was not a problem) and we were able to provide a full lunch as originally requested in the contract. We even found a limo service to bring everyone to/from the venue for their sit-down meal.

As a presenter, we know that we were treated to superstar quality in our little town. Michelle was gracious at all times, yet very down-to-earth. I also volunteer for our local Special Olympics Club. Two of our athletes presented flowers to her and the three of them sang "Silent Night" with the entire audience joining in. I don't think there was a dry eye in the house. It was so very touching—how can a small person have such a big heart? Thank you for treating everyone as though they were your personal friend, for spending so much time talking to your fans and signing the CDs, photos and T-shirts. This is what puts you in that elite category—a very tough act to follow.

Thank you for bringing a huge ray of sunshine into our lives. God bless you, Michelle. We wish you continued success and God's grace upon you. Nights like tonight makes it all worthwhile. My head will be full of memories each time I play Michelle's Christmas CD—each and every song a joy to listen to.

Sincerely,
Toni McInnes
Superior North Entertainment Series
Terrace Bay, ON

What a wonderful message. We're out here trying to touch people. This is what it's all about.

We'll stay in Manitouwadge overnight. As nice as the tour bus is, it's good to be sleeping in a bed that isn't moving.

November 21st

We played in Dorion this evening. It was probably the best show we've had. At the start of a tour, it takes a few days for a show to fall into place. We are all getting more relaxed, and we are now able to enjoy what we're doing without having to think about it as much.

We got seven kids sponsored. The sponsorship program is going well. We're all realizing now that we are part of something bigger than just a show playing town to town.

November 22nd

We have the day off, but we're traveling to Fort Frances. We'll be stopping at a music store in Thunder Bay for guitar repairs and supplies.

I had to hold some meetings today with everyone to discuss ways we can continue to tighten things up. These meetings, when we're on tour, most often occur in the back lounge of our bus, and are always difficult: we all have to examine where the weak links are, who needs to take responsibility for the problems, and how they can be tightened up. Sometimes these meetings can get a bit heated because ego gets in the way. But I've worked with all these guys for so long now, we're always able to work through whatever needs to be dealt with. I'm sure this time will be no exception.

I have a reception that I must attend tonight. I'm struggling with it because this is my night off and I could really use the rest, but I'm obligated to go. I'm sure I'll have a good time, but I'd rather hibernate in my room.

November 23rd

The reception last night was very nice. The organizers had visited my website and discovered that pizza was my favorite food. They had the biggest pizza delivered I have ever seen. That was very thoughtful. Now I'm feeling guilty that I didn't really want to go just because I was tired. Some of the group joined me, and we played darts and ate lots of pizza and had a fine time.

The show went great once again, and we got two kids sponsored. We drove on to Dryden after the gig.

November 24th

Not much to report tonight. The show here in Dryden went flawlessly. I guess the meeting in the back of the bus worked. That's not a surprise to me. These guys take a lot of pride in what they do, and they strive for excellence. Thanks, guys.

We got one child sponsored. It's a bit disappointing that we didn't get more, but what can you do?

We're staying here tonight.

November 25th

Another successful show tonight in Atikokan. We're running like a well-oiled machine.

We got four kids sponsored tonight. That's more like it.

Brad, my sound engineer and tour manager, is pretty sick.

He has a bad cold and not a lot of time to rest. His job is very demanding, so I always worry a bit when he gets sick out here on the road. You can't just shut the world off and rest in bed. We have a day off tomorrow. Hopefully, that will give him some time to rest and recover.

We're traveling to Chicago tomorrow. Sean's parents live there. They're going to prepare an American Thanksgiving dinner for us. We're all looking forward to that.

November 26th

Dinner at the Smith's was heartily appreciated by all of us. Some of the guys did their laundry while we were there. We then jumped back on the bus with our bellies full and went to our hotel rooms.

November 27th

The show in University Park, Illinois, was special. We performed in a beautiful performing arts center at Governors State University. Jeff Bates was our opening act. The concert was a fundraiser for the Chicago Area Families for Adoption (CAFFA) organization. The idea behind the event was to give kids and families whose lives were touched by adoption a special time to celebrate it through music with artists whose lives have also been touched by adoption. We were invited to participate because of "He Would Be Sixteen." That song was not based on any personal experience of mine, of course, but having gotten to know the Olanders over the past few years, I feel my life also has been somewhat touched by adoption. I have received many letters from people who shared their personal stories with me as a result of hearing "He Would Be Sixteen" on the radio. Their stories profoundly moved me.

While we were at the venue, a physical therapist friend of the promoter offered to look at my knee. He informed me that my kneecap had shifted because the muscle on the left side is weakened. He taped my knee in place and gave me some exercises to do. I couldn't believe the difference when he put my knee back into place. I'm sure glad I don't need surgery. I'll start with the exercises and hope that's all that'll be necessary.

Robbie O'Shea, the promoter, had thoughtfully arranged to have some massage tables set up backstage. I know that some of the boys indulged themselves. I went back to my hotel room and got ready for a dinner that the organizers had planned. They requested I be there to meet some of their VIPs, including some of the adopted kids and their families. Usually after sound check I go back to my room, order room service, rest, and get ready for the evening's show, but every situation is a little different. I was glad to attend the dinner.

We're driving to Nashville after the concert tonight. Needless to say, we're all looking forward to getting home for a few days before we head back up to Southern Ontario.

November 28th

Oh, there's no place like home. I rested a little bit and hung out with Marco and the dog and the cats.

We went to dinner at the Olander's. Our friend Mike Basow was also there with his parents. Mike's wife was going to come too, but she's six months pregnant and feeling a little bit under the weather, so she insisted that the rest go to the dinner without her. It was great to see everyone.

Jimmy and Claudia are building a new home. It's going to be so beautiful. I don't even know where to start in describing it. It will be a "smart house," very modern and run by a computer. It will even have heated floors. Now I know I have everything I need, but in my dreams, when Marco and I build our house together, it, too, will have heated floors.

Jimmy is putting a recording studio in the house and a cardio room for exercise. The Olanders will be a good source of information when we decide to build our house.

Their architect is one of Marco's best friends: Dave Powell. He's already let us know he'll help us do our design for our home. Jimmy and Claudia told us it's great to have a friend who's an architect because he knows you and he cares about you.

November 29th

I spent a full day listening to songs on Music Row. I don't think I heard any contenders.

Tonight, I took down all the Hallowe'en decorations inside the house and Marco took care of the outside. Then we got out all our Christmas decorations and I set to work. I really enjoy decorating the house at this time of the year, but I'm feeling sick and I've got to be careful because we still have a lot of touring to do. I worked until 1 a.m. and got a lot done.

November 30th

We bought our Christmas tree this morning. Marco and I are like two little kids when it comes to getting the tree. We always want the biggest one we can find (within reason). This year our tree is fifteen feet tall. I can't wait to decorate it. The room where the tree goes is twenty feet high, so a tall tree looks really beautiful when it's decorated and the lights are on. This is definitely one of our indulgences.

Debbie Zavitson and I went to three song meetings this afternoon. We heard a couple of good tunes. I didn't get home until 8 p.m. because I had some shopping I needed to do. Then I worked on the Christmas decorations until about 3 a.m. I know I'm overdoing it, but I want to get everything finished before I head back out on the road.

December 1st

I'm concerned about how sick I'm feeling. I should be in bed, but I can't be. I've got to get things done around here. Not getting my Christmas decorations up until the end of the tour in mid-December would be disappointing to me.

I'm reading this and realizing how foolish it all sounds. I'm sick, but I'm insisting on doing my decorations! I think this might be the last year I'll be able to do this; next year's tour is going to be bigger and longer. I'm lucky to have these days off to decorate this year.

Marco has been very helpful. Today is a beautiful day outside, a perfect day to finish the outdoor decorations.

Russ and Tony are doing some work on the album that doesn't involve me, some instrumental overdubs and such. I'll get to hear everything when I get back.

We leave at midnight for the last leg of the tour.

December 2nd

Our show tonight in Windsor went pretty well. When we started the show, I was afraid my voice was just not going to make it. The first few songs were a bit shaky, and I thought I was going to have to cancel the concert. But as I sang, my voice warmed up and got much better. Thank God. Canceling would have been a real drag.

Many family members were in the audience. It's the first time Mom has seen the Christmas show. My stepsister, Lesa, and my brother-in-law Henry came too. I don't see them very often, so I appreciated the effort they made to come and see me on the road.

We got two kids sponsored tonight.

December 3rd

Brian traveled on the bus with us to Windsor. This morning, he and I had a breakfast meeting with Mike Bowman from World Vision. Mike is in charge of their Artist Affiliate program. He seems very pleased with how well the program is going.

After our meeting, we checked out of our hotel. Brian, Sean, and I were driven to Sarnia to set up for tomorrow morning's TSC store opening. In Sarnia, Brian and I had dinner with three executives of a new booking agency, LiveTourArtists, who want to represent me in America. I enjoyed meeting the agents and appreciated their interest and enthusiasm. Change is always difficult, but sometimes it has to happen. I think I need to change to this agency for bookings in the States. I'll continue to digest our conversation, talk things over with Brian, and make a decision after some careful consideration.

Rui Da Silva, the producer of the *Women of Country*, called to say he was starting to solicit radio station interest in the show. He feels very positive about its potential. I'm excited about it, too.

Marco told me today that Claudia and Jimmy might not be able to adopt Tank (formerly known as Eli). They had thought the adoption was moving forward, so they changed his name, but now the young birth father is having second thoughts. This is a very challenging time for them: they've been fostering Tank since he was born and they've fallen in love with him.

We went to the TSC store at 9 p.m. to set up and do our sound check. I'm really tired and I'm concerned about my voice. I better get some sleep.

December 4th

I had a 6:30 a.m. wake-up call and an 8:00 a.m. pickup in the lobby. John Couper was there to drive us to the new TSC Store. It was good to see him again. We stopped at Tim Horton's for some breakfast, and then continued on to the store. We did our meet-and-greet with the TSC folks. I signed a *Wright Christmas* CD for each staff member and posed for pictures in front of a sleigh and Christmas tree that had been set up in the warehouse area especially for that purpose.

As usual, the store opening was fun and I signed autographs until after 1 p.m. Also in attendance were my Mom; Aunt Barb; my cousins Amy, Dezarae, and Amanda; my cousin Debbie; my grandparents, Art and Verla; and Julie, a good friend who has provided many pictures for the archives throughout the years. As tradition would have it, after we left the store we all went to Harvey's for burgers.

Next we drove to London to drop Brian off at the London

airport. He flew back to Nashville. Sean and I continued on to join the rest of the gang in Toronto for a private show for Honda Canada. Fortunately, I was able to get some rest in the back of the van; there were four thousand people at the show, and they came to have a good time. We rocked and the crowd did, too! They had their hands on the stage and sang and danced through the whole show. We all came off the stage sweating and feeling really pumped. After playing so many theaters where audiences tend to be more conservative, it was a nice change to blow it out tonight.

Ed, Lori, and Bryanna came and brought me back home to Barrie with them so I could have at least a few hours of family time.

My grandparents Verla and Art Ritchie.   Photographer: Julie Smith

December 5th

The drive from Toronto to Ed and Lori's is about an hour. I was very tired when we arrived around 11 p.m. last night. I put Bryanna to bed and read her a couple of stories. It didn't take her long to fall asleep. Once I climbed into bed, I was out like a light, too.

I slept in late because I really needed it. We just hung out and drank some coffee, and I played a bit with Bryanna. It was important that I had that time with her.

We left the house at 3 p.m. and drove to Parry Sound, the home of hockey legend Bobby Orr. Tonight's venue is called the Stockey Center. We played here last year. It was fun then, so we'll see how tonight goes.

My brother is coming to tonight's concert. This will be the first time that Ed, Lori, Bryanna, and Steve have seen the Christmas show.

We had a great show and got four kids sponsored. I like going out and signing autographs after the concert because it allows me to hear what people think of the show. This year's presentation has been going over very well. That makes me happy, of course, because when you put a show together you never know what the audience is going to think. So far, so good.

Marco went to a surprise birthday party for our dear friend Kerry Powell, the wife of Dave Powell the architect. Dave put together a video montage of Kerry's childhood as well as her performance on Star Search. She's a great soul singer. Marco said that Dave put a lot of work into the party and the video and that it was a fantastic time. I'm sorry I missed it.

After the show, on our way back to Nashville, the trailer got a flat tire. Its hydraulic jack was low in fluid, so the band and crew had to jump out and unload the trailer so they could jack it up and replace the tire. The weather was freezing, but the guys had fun with it and got the job done. I think after they thaw out it will be remembered as a bonding experience.

December 6th

We got home this afternoon. We'll be here for three days. I did laundry and got settled in. I'm feeling really good about how the tour is going. I'll be going to song meetings for the next couple of days.

Marco and I decided to put more lights in the backyard this year. Most of the lights are white and red, with a splash of blue. We decided to do our walkway around the back of the house in blue. The only problem is that the lights we bought for the backyard are a different color of blue than those in our front yard. Marco thinks it's fine, but I'm not happy with it. We're going to have to change this.

December 7th

Debbie Zavitson and I went to four listening sessions today. I don't feel like we heard anything great. It's like looking for a needle in a haystack, but that's just the way it goes.

Debbie and I are both dealing with colds. I'm trying to keep mine under control. I went to the gym this afternoon and sat in the sauna to try and sweat it out a bit.

December 8th

Debbie and I went to listen to songs again today. Another frustrating day. I'm trying to stay positive.

We're leaving again tomorrow, so I got a few things ready for the trip.

Marco is working until 10 p.m. every night. When he gets home at about 10:30 p.m., he's usually starving and I like to have something fixed for him to eat. It's pretty late to eat, but we're on a schedule that is different than usual.

December 9th

I did a little more Christmas decorating and got ready to leave. The bus pulled out of town at 3 p.m. We've got two shows tomorrow, and my cold is making me feel a bit low in energy. But I'll sleep today and tonight on the bus; hopefully, I'll feel better tomorrow.

December 10th

We played two shows today. Our first show was at 1 p.m.,

a private show in Markham for eight hundred Toronto-area auto dealers. Sometimes these private affairs can be pretty low-key, especially luncheon functions, but this one was really fun and the audience was very generous to us.

As soon as we were done, we had to load out and get on the road as quickly as we could. In the meantime, we had another crew setting up the second show for us in Peterborough. The logistics worked out flawlessly.

My songwriter friend Cyril Rawson lives in Peterborough. I invited Cyril and some of his friends to the concert. He enjoyed the show and it was nice to see him.

We got six kids sponsored.

December 11ᵗʰ

Our show at the Centrepointe Theatre in Ottawa went very well. It was snowing and freezing cold, but close to a thousand people still chose to leave the comfort of their homes and spend the night with us. Since it was the last show of the tour, it was nice to have such a good crowd. We're all

Photographer: Eric Bartnes

feeling really good about the tour, and, of course, everyone's looking forward to the holidays. We got seven kids sponsored. That's a good number to end the tour on.

It's always a bittersweet time when a tour finishes, but everyone is already talking about ideas for next year's Christmas tour.

I'm going to get home and finish my country CD. We can look forward to touring again in the spring.

December 12th

I woke up on the bus this morning feeling like I got hit by a truck. It's almost as though now the tour has ended, my body is finally shutting down. We got home safely and I climbed into bed. I need to get over this cold.

I'm feeling great about the tour.

Mom got home today. She had a good visit with Ed and Lori. She's glad she was able to spend some quality time with Bryanna, and she felt good about being helpful to Ed and Lori. They got a lot done while Mom was in Barrie, and now Ed and Lori are ready to open up shop in the new building.

December 13th

I listened to songs with Russ today. It's the first time we've attended listening meetings together. We heard some good songs, but, once again, I'm not sure that we heard any great songs.

Russ told me that Jo Dee Messina has recorded "My Give a Damn's Busted." That's a big disappointment. A song like that doesn't come along very often. I was thinking it might be my first single, but now we'll have to see. It's difficult to accept the fact that I just lost my first single, but this is where I just have to trust that all things happen for a reason.

Mom is working the Air Chair booth at the Bellevue Mall for Marco. Given its location, you'd think there would be more traffic there, but it's not doing very well. I imagine the mall will close down soon. This is Mom's first time selling Air

Chairs. I hope she doesn't get too discouraged.

Mom has to write exams for her Tennessee real estate license, so she is studying hard. This job in Bellevue will be something extra for her to do until she writes her test. Doing nothing is not my mother's specialty. She likes to work and has always been a highly-driven woman.

Marco is set up in three malls around Nashville this year. Having three booths gives him the opportunity to move more product and create some jobs at a time of the year when most people can use some extra money.

December 14th

I spent all day signing Christmas cards and getting gifts sent out to friends, family, and business associates.

I cooked a late dinner for Marco.

December 15th

More Christmas details. It's a good time to update my address book. There are always changes to be made and new addresses to add.

December 16th

Another day full of Christmas stuff. It's taking a long time to deal with all the odds and ends, but this is how it is every year. It takes time and you just have to put one foot in front of the other and get everything done.

December 17th

I shopped all day today for Christmas gifts. Then I managed to send off all our presents for family in Canada. I made it to the post office just in time before it closed for the weekend. I staggered in with seventy-five cards and a variety of boxes that needed mailing. The look on the post office worker's face was telling. He thought his day was almost over until I came stumbling in with things going out to a variety of countries. I needed stamps for this and forms for that. He gave me a little attitude at first, but then he apologized. I told him I understood. I can just imagine the endless flow of people coming into the post office at this time of year. It feels good to have that task completed.

December 18th

Today, I spent a full day finishing the Christmas decorations outside. Marco notwithstanding, I finally changed the blue lights on the walkway to red, and it looks great. Kmart took back all the blue lights that didn't match. I had to put them in garbage bags because we had thrown out the packaging, but the store took them back anyhow.

I also cleaned out the garage. I know it seems like I clean out the garage a lot, but every couple of months it needs to be dealt with.

Things are in order and our Christmas decorations look great. I'm filled with the Christmas spirit. I'm feeling the best I've felt for a while. That cold really hung on, but it finally seems to be going away.

December 19th

We slept in this morning. Marco has people working for him today. I'm really happy because that means we can spend the whole day together. We went to the late church service and had a nice quiet day.

December 20th

I sent away a few more Christmas gifts and cards for business and friends. I made a lot of phone calls to my business associates as well. Next I have to shop for Christmas presents for Marco and Mom.

I'm quite confused by the fact that some people want to take Christ out of Christmas. I don't understand that at all. Maybe I'm missing something here, but isn't Christmas a celebration of the birth of Christ?

December 21st

I had a lot of fun shopping for Mom and Marco today. I came home and wrapped everything and put the gifts under the tree. That pretty much took all day.

I made another late dinner for Marco. I'm counting down the days until he is done working for the season. Marco has agreed to let Mom put Blaze, the nephew of another Bellevue shop owner, in charge of her Air Chair booth while she takes a few shifts for Marco at his Cool Springs Mall location. Marco has been working almost every day since November 23. Breaking up some of those twelve-hour shifts he's been working will be good.

December 22nd

I had just a little more Christmas shopping to do. Marco has dropped a few hints about things he'd like for Christmas. Thank God for that, because it's hard to buy for him.

December 23rd

The gifts are purchased and the decorating is done! Now I need to plan the dinner for Christmas Day. I'm so excited that the holidays are here.

December 24th

I went shopping for all the ingredients for our traditional Polish Christmas meals. I readied everything for the oven tomorrow. We'll be having borscht, cabbage rolls, pierogies, Polish sausage and sauerkraut, as well as ice cream, and apple and pumpkin pie.

Marco worked until 6 p.m. and now it's holiday time. We all went to Christmas service at the church and then went to a party at Bob and Patricia's, but we didn't stay out too late.

December 25th

What a great Christmas! We got up, had coffee, and opened up all of our presents. Marco got Mom and me a day at the spa. I can't wait for that pampering. Then it was time for palacsinta. It is so good. I put all the prepared Polish food in the oven, and we rested and watched *It's a Wonderful Life* while dinner cooked.

All the food turned out just the way it should. Mmmm... Life is good.

December 26th

Marco worked at Cool Springs Mall all day. I cleaned house and rested.

December 27th

Marco and I took down the booth in Bellevue. Then we went to a couple of stores and exchanged some of the stuff we got for Christmas.

In the evening, we went out for dinner at Antonio's, a really nice Italian restaurant just around the corner from where we live. This was the first time we'd gone there together. Marco gives it two thumbs up.

December 28th

I listened to songs at home today in preparation for a song meeting with Russ, Tony, and Brian tomorrow. I also tried to set up some songwriting appointments for January, but everyone has pretty much "shut her down for the season." We're going into the studio January 21 to finish the rest of the bed tracks for my country CD.

After all our work was done, Marco and I got into our pajamas in the afternoon and watched *Elf* and mellowed out. The movie was cute and certainly appropriate for the season. I think Will Ferrell is pretty funny.

December 29th

Brian, Tony, Russ, and I had our song meeting today. I'm not sure how I'm feeling, though a couple of songs have caught my attention. One song that Debbie and I found early on, but the guys weren't sure of, has come to the forefront again. I really like it. It's called "Ridin' Around the Sun." Tony and Russ really like another song called "So Close." It's a spoken song with only the choruses being sung. I like it, too. Another song that's been circulating around town for a while is called "Dance in the Boat." Tony wrote it a few years ago. Of course, I'm a big fan of his writing, so it would be great to record another one of his songs.

The bad news for today is that Jo Dee Messina has indeed released "My Give a Damn's Busted," as a single. That's a tough pill to swallow, but there's nothing I can do about it. On the other hand, she also recorded "Dance in the Boat," but didn't end up putting it on her record. Maybe she'll have a hit with "My Give a Damn's Busted" and I'll have a hit with "Dance in the Boat."

This evening, Tony and his wife, Julia, hosted a really nice dinner for Russ and Debbie, Brian and his wife, Sue, and Marco and me. Earlier in the day Marco had put his back out at the gym, and he wasn't sure if he'd be able to come. I was very disappointed. This was the first opportunity we'd had to get all of us together. Marco obviously didn't do it on purpose, and I was trying to be understanding. When I came home from the song meeting, I tried not to show my disappointment. But Marco knew how important this was to me, so he decided that as long as he could sit a certain way, his back wouldn't hurt too badly.

We had a fun night together. Lots of good food, good conversation, lots of laughs. Tony played a song he recently finished, called "Who Da' Baby Daddy?" It's a Christmas parody and it's brilliant. You know, there's something very special about being able to sit around the table and hear great music performed live by the writer. I'm thankful we were all able to get together this evening.

December 30th

Marco rested in bed so his back could heal. I took care of

him, and kept busy with the daily household routine.

December 31st

We had a party for New Year's Eve and had lots of fun. Our friend Colette Wise got engaged tonight. We're very happy for her. I don't know her fiancé all that well, but the couple of times I've hung out with him, I've gotten a good feeling about him. I know Colette is happy. He is a doctor named Dan Bercu, and he does missions throughout the year in Third World countries. That says a lot about his character right there. Here comes another wedding.

We watched the ball drop in Times Square without Dick Clark this year. Apparently, he's had a stroke. I'm sorry to hear that. We toasted the new year and partied until 4 a.m.

Well, that's it. One year in my life. My, how time flies! As I look back and review the year, I'm very happy with how most things went.

My weight fluctuated and once again I'm starting a new year with the hope that this time I can maintain a better balance in my workout routine.

I had a good year of touring.

I'm glad that my Christmas CD turned out as well as it did. The process of making *A Wright Christmas* surprised me. It was easy and fun. I guess that's because we weren't looking for a hit. All I had to worry about was singing some standards to the best of my ability.

Working with Russ and Tony was the right choice for me. We had a good time making music we enjoy. I have a lot of respect for the experience they bring to the craft. They supported me in my choice of songs. The bottom line is that I'm the one who has to sing these songs night after night with conviction. My approach to recording is not about acting, but rather singing about what I have experienced and what I understand. I wish we could have finished my country CD, but we'll get it done first thing in the new year.

Writing songs for the country album has proven to be very challenging. The bad news is that after all the hard work I put in with my co-writers this past year, I may have only a couple of my own songs on the CD. The good news, however, is that Nashville is full of some of the best songwriters in the world, and I have the privilege of recording their songs. Producer Buddy Cannon once said that finding the right songs for an artist is always the biggest challenge, no matter who the artist is. He said that if you put a good singer on an OK song, then what you have in the end is still just an OK song. Finding the best songs is a demanding part of the process, but you just have to keep on digging. I feel really good about the choices of songs we've made to date, but only time will tell if I'm creating music that will allow me to sustain what we've achieved so far or take my career to another level. None of us know what will happen, but I do believe anything is possible.

I'm glad the *Women of Country* is being well received by radio stations. I appreciate the opportunity to use my speaking voice for a change.

My activity with World Vision continues to be something that I find purposeful. I'm so thankful I can take my career and use it to help other people.

The TSC gang? You're incredible!

There's been more than a few weddings this year in our circle. And a few babies as well. For Marco and me, the conversation continues.

I'm so glad Mom moved to Nashville. I love having her here.

I love my Marco more than ever. I think we both agree: "It's a wonderful life."

P.S. Gracie and the cats say "Happy New Year" too.

Acknowledgments

Thanks to publisher Mike O'Connor for helping me create another way to connect with my audience. Thanks as well to Maria Bruk Auperin and Daniel Varrette at Insomniac Press for your skillful copy editing and positive feedback.

I would like to especially acknowledge my personal manager, Brian Ferriman, and my business manager, Sue Ferriman. In this, our 20th year together as a team, Brian, my respect for you continues to grow, and your guidance throughout the process of writing these journals is greatly appreciated. To Sue, much respect to you as well, and thanks for keeping things in order for me.

To my road band and crew, Lee Warren, (band leader, steel guitar, lead and slide guitar, web designer), Dan Nadasdi (piano and keyboards), Sean Smith (lead guitar), Rick Marks (drummer), Brad Burkett (road manager, sound engineer) and Eric Bartnes (lighting director): I'm thankful that you all share your unique talents with me, and I also think you're pretty cool guys! Love to my wonderful circle of friends who fill my life with joy and support. To all of my family: I love you very much. To my husband Marco: you have brought a light into my life that surpasses all I had hoped for. And last, but not least, to the people who have supported my music, driven to my concerts, applauded, stood up and asked for more: thank you. You have made my dreams come true.